MW00565155

The Author

Chasing My Dreams

The Fritz Lang Story

Fritz Lang

ISBN 978-1-63575-984-6 (paperback)
ISBN 978-1-64114-898-6 (hardcover)
ISBN 978-1-63575-985-3 (digital)

Copyright © 2017 by Fritz Lang

Christian Faith Publishing, Inc.
832 Park Avenue
Meadville, PA 16335
www.christianfaithpublishing.com

Printed in the United States of America

Dedication

D ear reader: This is Volume One of my story, and an even more exciting volume will be coming your way next—Volume Two. I thank you for taking the time to read this book and hope to keep you interested in the next installment. This Volume One is dedicated to my dear mother, born Anna Maria Eberlein, on August 19, 1907. She was the rock and backbone of our family. Not only did she have six kids, but she took care of all of us like no other mother that I knew of. A special thanks to my sister Liselotte who supported me with her literate knowledge throughout the book.

Foreword
by Walter Engelke

One of my earliest childhood memories is of my Uncle Fritz. It was the latter part of the 1960's and my Mother took me for a walk from our apartment in New Rochelle to the local Marina where her brother Fritz was building a houseboat. I could not have been older than five. Uncle Fritz was working on his boat and saw us on shore and started waving and yelling out my name to greet me. I'm certain it put a huge smile on my face and it has been a pleasure and adventure knowing him ever since. All I really can attest to from those earlier days is that my Uncle always had a nice looking car and a nice looking girlfriend and sometimes if I was lucky I was invited to join them for a drive. Over all the years since then I have had so many clear and wonderful memories of him that I cannot possibly start to tell you about them because it would become a new book all by itself. All I can say is this amazing book traces the history of my Uncle's childhood and all the events that eventually brought him to both America and to me—and we are both the more fortunate because of it.

I t is a warm summer morning here in Dutchess County, and I am dressed only in shorts. Even the slightest movement causes sweat to run in rivulets down my body. It is early yet, but the sun is already strong, so I move to sit under the umbrella. A light breeze comes in from the northwest from the nearby spring-fed lake, moving across the lawn and onto the porch. My house here in Beekman is surrounded by large trees. The pine and the mighty native oak trees give us a sense of security and a nice shelter.

And the lake, called Sylvan Lake, was carved out of a glacier back in the Ice Age. It is the deepest and second-largest lake in the County. The American Indians called it Lake Apoquaque, which means "round water." In the 1700s, it was Wiltzies Pond, then Roger Pond, Poughaquag Pond, Silver Lake, and then in 1876, it got its current name.

The bird's eye view of the lake is that of an irregular oval of 114 acres. At the deepest point, it is about 138 feet, and it flows northwest, draining into a three-acre pond, and from there southward to Fishkill Creek, finally emptying into the Hudson River at the City of Beacon. Just being near the lake relaxes me. The water is so clear people claim you can drink it. No boats with gasoline engines are allowed on the lake. I like to go out in my rowboat, which has an electric motor, or in my kayak. In the winter, the lake often freezes over, and it is wonderful to ice skate in the moonlight under a clear sky.

It is Monday morning and I decide to begin my life story. I move inside and take a seat in front of my computer. Time is everything and time will tell us what I am capable of.

It is summer 1943 and we live in Wiesbaden-Biebrich in a part of the city called Gibb. It is a well-known area because of the Gibber fairgrounds, which were built in 1909. Because I was born on July 3, the same day as the Gibber Fair, I feel I have always been connected to the fair.

There were six children in our family—in 1943 I was five, my youngest sister Liselotte was four, my brother Joseph was seven, and my sister Marianne was eight. The four of us lived with our mother in the Gibb, and our father was away in the war. World War II was in full swing, and everyone of age had to go fight. My twin sisters Erika and Ingeborg, who were just thirteen at the time, lived in the Hammermuehle ("English Hammer Mill") with Grandma and Grandpa Trapp, my maternal grandparents.

Our house was a two-story English Tudor at the corner of Weihergasse 9 and Bachgasse. It had a garden and a three-feet-high concrete retaining wall on the street side. The garden was higher than the street and the front yard. Along the cement wall was a three-foot-high wooden fence, and a few steps down gave onto the lower front yard. You entered the front yard and then in to the house from the street side via a wooden door, which was connected through a post and frame with a double barn door.

You couldn't see into the front yard from the street side. Since 1943 was a hot and humid summer, Mother would fill a galvanized tin tub so we kids could splash naked in the tub in the front yard. One day when I was five, I accompanied Mother when she went to a cabinetmaker's shop. As soon as I inhaled the smell of the freshly cut wood, I told her I wanted to be a cabinetmaker when I grew up. And ten years later, I became an apprentice in a cabinetmaker's workshop.

from left to right in back Inge, mother, Marianne, Erika, Liselotte my
father in front Josef and myself Fritz. The picture was taken in 1943

The Deadly War

I remember how frequently we would hear the air sirens at night, warning us of incoming fighter planes which were extremely low-flying military aircraft. Everyone would run in terror to the closest shelter for safety. It was common for those who came last to bring along various items of clothing that one of us had dropped in the rush.

One night I remember well, I was in the outhouse when the sirens began to scream and I had to run with my pants pulled halfway up as our entire family raced to the bunker. We had some very close calls, sometimes so close that we didn't make it out of the house when the sirens sounded. We could hear the deadly screams from nearby homes. And bombs dropping all around us. On those wretched nights, millions of Germans died, women and children alike, all over Germany, with no regard for nationality or faith. When day broke, you could see the devastation from the night before: houses totally destroyed, streets ripped apart so the rescue squad and fire department could not reach the homes to save any lives or buildings. Eventually, Mother decided that we had to leave the city. We fled to the country, to Bavaria, the hometown of my father, Thurn Heroldsbach.

The Kindergarten Prison

When it was possible, we attended school and or kindergarten a few hours a day. I remember one day very clearly: we had a new young female teacher who was very strict and made all us kids hold hands as we walked in the schoolyard. But I disobeyed her, and I was punished: she locked me up in a storage room. All the other kids left the building, as did the teachers. I was left alone in a dark 6x3-foot janitor's closet for about four hours until the cleaning woman got there. She came to get cleaning supplies and found me locked in the closet. It was dumb luck. It happened to be a Friday afternoon, which was the day she cleaned; otherwise, I would have been imprisoned until the following Monday without food or water. The cleaning lady delivered me safely to my house. My mother was so upset over this incident that she reported it to the authorities in the city. I believe that was the last we saw of that young teacher in my classroom—my mother saw to it that she was put in a different kindergarten.

Our Daily Bread and a Bath on the Weekend

On Fridays, the delivery man from the local bakery came with a single horse-drawn, closed wagon to deliver bread and other baked goods to many families throughout the city. Our mother got about six loaves at once at the time, which were usually rye. They were about five inches wide, three inches high, sixteen inches long, and rounded on the top and the ends. We stored the bread on top of the free-standing cabinet in the bedroom, and it lasted a week or two without refrigeration (in the 1940s and '50s, the average German household did not have refrigeration). The bedrooms had no heat, so they were the coolest place in the house.

On the weekend, everyone had to take a bath, especially in the summer. We kids were twice as dirty in the summers because we dressed only in shorts, t-shirts, and we didn't wear shoes. It took quite a while for all of us to bathe. First, we heated the water on the coal stove, and then filled the portable tin tub. The process began in the late afternoon when the youngest was bathed and then put to bed. Each time a child was bathed, we then emptied the dirty water in the courtyard where there was a drain in between the cobblestones. And then the whole process started again until all were bathed and put to bed. Since most people did not have built-in bathrooms in those days, it took an hour to get ready between the bathing and dressing. In the later years, there was a public bathhouse, and I remember the pleasure of going there to bathe.

Children in the Garden

O ne day, my sister and I were playing in the garden
and we heard irregular footsteps coming towards
us down the cobblestone sidewalk. We looked
in amazement as we saw a black woman coming toward
us. She was using a cane because she had a lame leg. As
she came closer, we hid behind a bush. As she came limp-
ing past our garden, a cold shiver came over us. We had
never seen a black person in our entire life. We only knew
them from the storybooks we read. So we really thought
that this woman might be a witch. As soon as she passed,
we ran into the house and locked the door behind us. As
we peeked through the window, we saw her moving down
the street, and then she was gone. After the war, Germany
was packed with Black American soldiers, and we quickly
learned that the only difference between black and white
people was the color of the skin.

On another day, all of us were playing in the garden
including my older sister Marianne and my brother Josef.
We were playing with matches and suddenly the hay in
the open barn caught fire. Luckily, there wasn't much hay
in the barn, only enough for our rabbits, and they were in
a separate stall next to the barn. It was a lot of excitement
for one day, but the fire was quickly extinguished and there
was no major damage. Now when I think back on it, I real-

ize that my poor mother had her hands full with all of us kids. She worked in the fields with the farmers so we had food to eat, and her only transportation was a bicycle for all the chores, including shopping.

The Telegram

Near the end of the summer in 1944, Mother received a telegram from Father requesting that she come see him in Karlsruhe. Father was in charge of about one hundred Russian war prisoners who had been captured by the Germans towards the end of the war. They were kept in a fenced compound outside of Karlsruhe in a town called Durlach. It was out in the country, and the prisoners worked in the fields and forests; no one escaped from Father's compound.

Mother took me with her and also took Ingeborg, one of my older sisters. We traveled by train to Karlsruhe and took the street car to Durlach. After we arrived in Durlach, we boarded a funicular (Bergbahn), a mountain railway on tracks which was pulled by cable and counterweight—the downward car pulls the uphill car to the top (there was also an electric motor). The railway was put in service in 1888 and is the second oldest in Germany, running daily from 10:00 a.m. until 20:00 p.m. When we got to the top, a horse-drawn carriage took us to our final destination, an estate on a large compound. It was built in a horseshoe formation of solid masonry, with one end facing the fields. All stalls, barns, and living quarters faced a large courtyard. Here there were no air attacks or sirens to worry about, and the people were very friendly. We had food that we had never tasted before.

The next morning after breakfast, we visited Father in the prison camp and he showed us all around and gave me same wooden toy airplanes that the Russian prisoners had made. This was the first toy I remember getting in a very long time. My sister and I went with the farmhands in the fields to make hay. We sat in a large horse-drawn wooden wagon full to the top and everyone had to climb on top of the hay.

Much later, my father told me that at the end of 1944, he was released from his duties as a prison warden and sent to the Russian front like all other soldiers. He was caught shortly after by the Russians as were many German soldiers and ended up a Russian prisoner of war. After our one week stay, we had to go back home to the rest of the family. It wasn't easy to leave such a peaceful place where we had had so much leisure. While we were away, my brother and three sisters had stayed with my aunt who had five kids of her own. My aunt's husband worked in a factory that used a lot of coal, and the family actually lived in the backyard of the factory. Years later, my sister Liselotte still remembers the ordeal of being exposed to all that coal dust. My brother Joseph and my older sister Marianne stayed with our other Aunt, and my sister Erika stayed with our grandmother. We were reunited and happy to be alive. Besides the toy airplanes my father had given me, we brought eight walnut tree saplings, which we planted in our garden in Biebrich.

The Journey to Bavaria

We boarded at night in Wiesbaden-Biebrich, the east train station to Frankfurt on the River Main. As we arrived in Frankfurt, we had to change trains, and the train in Frankfurt was packed with German soldiers traveling to the front. At one point during the journey, I had to go to the toilet, but there was no way I could get through the mass of people and reach the bathroom. The train was packed and the windows were open for ventilation, so one of the soldiers lifted me up so I could piss out of the window of the moving train.

Halfway through our journey, the train came to a sudden stop and all of us had to disembark. Low-flying planes were approaching. Most people crawled under the train and so did Mother with us kids. After a little while, we got out from under the train and took cover in a nearby bunker. My mother followed the rest of the people but somehow, I got lost. I don't know what happened, but I remember running over the lawn up a hill screaming for my mother. One of the soldiers pushed me down as the bombs came raining down around us. I still remember getting up again and screaming for my mother and running across the lawn towards the bunker. The whole operation was over before I knew what was going on.

By then, I was totally exhausted from running and screaming. I must have screamed my lungs out in this ordeal, and all around me were dead bodies and badly wounded people—women, children and soldiers alike. Finally, I was reunited with my family and after the cleanup, we continued on our journey late the same night. After we arrived in Nuernberg, the train changed to a much slower local train. There were no more soldiers in our compartment and the train was not very full at all. We were completely exhausted and the journey continued into the early morning hours of the following day. Half asleep and half awake, we finally reached our destination—Oma's (Grandma's) place. It was a one-street town with one restaurant at the end of the street. Thurn was nothing more than a street with only farmers. All other businesses like the baker, grocery, hardware store, church, and post office were found next door in Heroldsbach.

Our Stay in Bavaria

After we arrived in Bavaria, everything was new and unusual for the first few days. Grandmother Lang was my paternal grandmother, a woman in her late fifties, with a large, rugged frame. Most of her teeth were missing. She had given birth to seven strong, healthy boys. In the photo on page 20, they are lined up from left to right: Michael, Hans, Georg, Andreas, Josef, Konrad, and the youngest, Ludwig, who is seated in front between my great-grandmother and my grandmother. At the time we arrived, they all were away in the war. If they hadn't been, there would not have been enough room for everyone to stay at my grandmother's house. My Uncle Ludwig's wife and her two girls Renate and Margitte were also living there.

Generally, it was a peaceful place. There were no low-flying airplanes as the war was going strong in another part of the country. Grandmother Lang made her own bread. She always made two round loaves about twenty inches (fifty-one centimeters) in diameter. Since she had no stove big enough for those loaves, she went to the local baker and left the bread to be baked. She transported the bread one and a half miles on a wheelbarrow covered with a board on which she placed the loaves.

But we did experience a big disruption when we were there. I remember that my mother received a telegram informing her that our home in Biebrich had been totaled and she had to go back to put the furniture in storage. When she got back to Gibb, she discovered that the only thing left was the furniture and some bricks and mortar dust. People had taken the lumber for firewood. The only saving grace of the trip was that she made it back in one piece. In those days, it wasn't easy to stay alive.

Grandma's house was at Thurn 50—that was the address in the family for generations. It was a two-story stucco building with a stable and a barn. We had two pigs, a cow, and some geese and chickens. The barn was a big building that sat across the yard, and the water supply came from a hand-dug well in the middle of the yard. We didn't have running water. For some, there was a mechanism that was a tripod with rollers, but in our case, you had to grab a pail on a line and pull it hand over hand. At the back of the house, there were four connecting ponds that contained fish.

In fact, the ponds belonged to the local Graf, or Earl, as they say in Britain. In Thurn, there was a big park with a castle, where the countess and her son lived. The count was away in the war like all the other men. Since some of the farmland belonged to the count, it was the custom that the local farmers delivered bread, milk, meat, and all the other products that the farm produced. There was another custom: the women of the royal family did not breast-feed their babies—that task was taken on by local women. It fell to my grandmother, who had given birth to seven healthy boys, to be the wet nurse to the countess.

When my father was a young man, before I was born, he sold horseradish in Wiesbaden. He would pack up two large suitcases and travel by railway from Thurn Heroldsbach to Wiesbaden, and go house to house selling the horseradish. It turned out that this was how he met my mother. According to him, it was love at first sight. They were married in Biebrich in the Roman Catholic Church, even though my mother was Lutheran. In those days it was common for any offspring to take the father's religion.

In 1944, I started the first grade in a school in Bavaria. It was a peaceful place for everyone, and we kids played freely on the street and in the yard. The streets were made of dirt and gravel, since the only traffic would be a farmer with his horse and wagon. Since we were newcomers in town, people were curious about who we were and what our names were. I told them our name was Lang, and that seemed to mean nothing to them. Only after I pointed to the house would they nod and say, "Oh, you're the Adelschuster Sepper kids." That translates to "royal shoemaker." "Sepper" is my father's name, Joseph, so people only knew the name that had been given long ago, not our actual family name.

In the fall, my grandmother went into the forest with a woven basket on her back to collect branches as kindling for the fire in the stove. We kids would go along to help her collect the branches. The winter of 1944 to 1945 was a very cold one, and it snowed almost every other day. There were no snow plows then, but the local traffic packed down the snow a bit, and we kids played in it as much as we could.

There were two kitchens in the house—one in which they prepared food for the animals, and there was an oven that heated the whole house. The kitchen and living room had a common wall with a built-in *Kachelofen* (clay stove), which was made of shiny green clay tiles with baked enamel on the outside. The oven was four feet deep by six feet long and extended from floor to ceiling with a metal grill that allowed the heat to radiate through and heat the tiles. There was a built-in bench, so the women could sit there at night and do their knitting.

Grandma was Roman Catholic and my mother was Lutheran, Grandma sprinkled holy water every time my mother left the room. She kept a porcelain vase hanging on the wall next to the door, which was filled with holy water to keep the devil at bay. People of different religious faiths didn't really coexist in those days. Most people's minds were made up on those matters, and it was a given that there was only one correct or valid religion: the one you believed in.

My Uncle Georg married a well-educated and wealthy lady from the big city, Munich, and they built a very nice two-story brick house right next door to my grandmother's house. His house had a new modern kitchen with running water and a tiled bathroom with a bathtub and regular toilet, the only one in town. The woman who rented the house from my uncle worked from home with healing medicinal herbs. The townspeople didn't like her and called her a witch and a quack, since she had no degree. We kids liked her and she was good to us. On rare occasions, she let one of us kids stay in the house overnight. I recall one night that I stayed there, I had to go to the toilet, and after I was finished, I did not flush because I did not want to wake her up, so I got a lecture the next day about making sure to always flush.

In the winter months, the nights were long and very cold, and Granny's house was freezing, especially our rooms which were on the upper floors. We had warm underwear and blankets, but the single-pane windows were frozen all winter long until springtime. On windy nights, you could hear the wind cut right through the gaps between the windows and the old wooden frames. Mother would wrap a hot brick in a towel and put it in bed with us to help keep us warm.

At Christmas, we didn't get toys because the war was still going on, and all factories and workshops were geared up to produce wartime goods. After the long cold winter, the spring of 1945 finally arrived. The snow melted away and the green buds on the bushes and trees came out to stay, at least for a while.

The big news was that the war was over and the Americans were coming soon. In many towns, the Hitler youth, usually between twelve and sixteen years old, were still defending their towns. Since they were not soldiers anymore, they had been captured and were now prisoners of war. Many of them were missing in action, as my father and his six brothers were. Of the seven young men, only three came home alive after the war.

As the day of the Americans' arrival drew near, the women panicked and told horrible stories about the American military. There was vicious gossip about black soldiers raping women and cutting off their breasts. The panic was at an all-time high. I remember that when my grandmother got word that the Americans were coming, she gathered up all the silver crosses and other military medals and decorations from the war and threw them in the pond. They are still there today because the bottom of the pond is nothing but mud, and so it isn't likely anyone could ever find them.

My mother kept her cool, and told everyone to go to the basement of the castle, which had been designated as a shelter during the war. That is just what they did. She told them, "I will feed your animals so you can stay in a safe place." My mother hung a white sheet out the second floor window facing the direction from which the soldiers were expected to march into town. I was with her at the time because I felt safe being with her, and I remember the American infantry marching in on the back side of the house across the pond around noon on this spring day.

They did a house-to-house inspection for the safety of the troops. We had to stay off the streets for a few days until they were settled in their new accommodations. They took the best places in town, and I believe they took over the castle for a short time as their headquarters. In the end, everything was fine and the farm women returned with no one suffering any harm.

After a while, my mother talked about leaving Bavaria and going home to Wiesbaden-Biebrich. It was the beginning of summer and the Americans, French, English, and the Russians were occupying all of Germany, so it was a good time to get back to our hometown. The only thing that kept us from leaving was that we didn't have the right papers to travel to our hometown. But Mother would not let bureaucracy hold her back and planned to leave Thurn Heroldsbach as soon as possible. She knew the train was not an option because all public transportation was completely shut down since the Allies had come to Germany.

She decided that we would walk from Thurn Heroldsbach to Wiesbaden-Biebrich. It was about 350 kilometers (217.5 miles), a big undertaking since we were only five, six, eight, and nine years old. The first item we needed was a wooden handcart to carry our belongings. We were able to get one through our local pastor at the church. The cart was about four feet long and thirty inches wide with a long handle so that two people could pull the wagon and steer the front wheels. The wheels were made of wood and were about eighteen inches in diameter with a steel rim. The bed was solid hardwood and the sides were made of oak spindles like a ladder, which could be removed for easy loading.

A Twelve-Day Journey

We planned to leave on June 14. My older sister Marianne had to say goodbye to her girlfriends. The rest of us were too young to have any close acquaintances. Our journey started in the early morning, with my sister Marianne and my brother Joseph in front pulling the wagon and my sister Liselotte, only five, sitting on top of our belongings. My mother and myself were in the back pushing as the journey began.

At lunchtime, we took a rest in a wooded area just next to a pond. We all took off our shoes and waded in the refreshing water to cool off our feet before resuming our journey. There were no hotels, so we stayed in a field and got a good night's rest.

My brother Joseph's birthday is on July 14, so he says that he remembers June 14 well—his birthday was just four weeks away. In the afternoon, we were pushing our wagon uphill through a city called Erlangen as a caravan of U.S. soldiers drove by in open trucks. The soldiers waved to us, and one of them tossed a Hershey bar to us kids. Since we were pulling and pushing the wagon uphill, we couldn't grab it and it landed on the sidewalk. An elderly lady raced out of her house and snatched it. This would have been the first chocolate of our lives, and if we had gotten our hands on it, we would have shared it among all of us, since we were brought up to share. The day was not all bad, though, as we found a family outside of town who took us in for the night; we had a good night sleep. The woman's husband and two sons were still not home from the war, so there was room for us. In the morning she and her daughter gave us oatmeal and coffee. The coffee was caffeine-free—that's all you could get at the time, and there was no milk or juice in those days.

June 15, Day 2

I remember that as we got started, we had to detour through a field and a forest since our passports had been issued during the war and were no longer valid. The Allies had established checkpoints at the entrances and exits to the cities and towns. If you were stopped, they took you to a camp where there were hundreds of families in one big hall, and transported you back where you came from.

June 16, Day 3

The day started out just fine. It was rather cloudy, so we could walk many miles without breaking a sweat. We put in mile after mile, keeping as much as possible to the countryside because of the checkpoints set up by the Allies. We had to sleep in a barn outside of town since there was no way to get into town without getting stopped by the British soldiers. In the morning, we had no water to wash up and no breakfast either, but Mother had some fruit and nuts from our last stop, and we always had drinking water.

June 17, Day 4

We got a good start and the weather was on our side. Around noon, we got to Ansbach and had to go to the outskirts of town again, keeping to the countryside and forested areas. As we walked along through the forest, Mother noticed that some men were hiding in the woods and they started running after us. She told us to run, and you should have seen us take off running for our lives, wagon and all. After a while, it seemed like we were losing ground since the wagon held us back. We had been told that the men from the Eastern bloc of Europe were out to kill Germans for what had happened during the war. We must have ran about a half hour nonstop until we finally came to a main road. Just as we made it out of the field and into the street, a wheel came off the wagon. We were in the open, so there was no danger anymore. As we inspected the damaged wagon, a military truck stopped. The soldiers were British and they spoke English. They loaded us kids, the wagon, and Mother into the truck and took off with us.

The truck ride only lasted about thirty minutes. It was a shaky ride because of the cobblestones. The soldiers got down, opened the back gate and started to unload the truck: first, the kids and then our mother, and then our broken wagon. To our surprise, we discovered that we were in a town. One of the soldiers had taken us to his girlfriend's house. This young lady helped us by putting us up with various villagers. Each of us got put up with a family, and we got to clean up and have a meal. They took the wagon to a blacksmith shop to get it fixed. We slept very well that night as we were exhausted from running for our lives earlier that day.

June 18, Day 5

In the morning we felt great after a good breakfast, and we were reunited with the rest of the family. We had to wait for the wagon to be repaired, so we got a later start. After we loaded the wagon, we started our new adventure about 10:00 a.m. and the young lady from the night before walked with us through the checkpoint of the town so we could get through the border controls without any passport or papers. She spoke English and she explained that we were going to the local mill with our bags of oats to have them milled. Forty-three years later, I went back to this town—it was called Rothenburg ob der Tauber, a historic town founded in 1274 that is enclosed by a fifteen-foot-high stone wall, the best preserved medieval town in all of Germany.

Day 5 went pretty well: we had a sandwich from our last stop and some fruit and plenty of water. Our mother always kept a loaf of bread in our travel bag if possible, along with fruit and nuts and a jug of water. After lunch, we continued our journey to Heidelberg, then came to a town called Bad Wimpfen. Because we got stopped because our passports had expired, we had to wait for a pickup. It was so late and the last pickup had just left, so we went to find a place to sleep.

June 19, Day 6

The next morning, we got an early start as always. Our new goal was to reach Heidelberg. It seemed that the closer we got to our goal, the better the journey. We reached Heidelberg am Neckar and got a place by an older couple right below the Grand Castle, which had been almost totally bombed out.

June 20, Day 7

The couple from the night before asked us to stay an extra day so we set out to see the sights and we got a rest from walking with the wagon.

June 21, Day 8

We started out well-rested and full of hope that we would see our Wiesbaden-Biebrich soon. We still tried to stay in the fields and away from the main road, but the inspections were winding down and the soldiers had better things to do. We stayed over in Mannheim in an old, bombed-out hotel. It was a wild night. There were no windows left in the frames but structure gave us shelter from the elements. Because it was summertime, that was fine with us. There was no running water, so we made a stop outside town at a farm.

June 22, Day 9

We ran into traffic on the route to Worms, but the days were not too long. We were almost there and Mother allowed us an easier pace. We arrived in Worms and found a place in a barn with the farmer's permission. We laid our clothes over the hay to get a good night's sleep. In the morning, the farmer's wife let us wash up and gave us eggs for breakfast—that was the first time in a long while we'd had any eggs, and we didn't have them again for a long time after.

June 23 Day 10

We made our way to Bad Kreuznach and the day was pretty uneventful.

June 24 Day 11

We mainly traveled on backroads to avoid the checkpoints, so we didn't see the extent of the destruction of the cities. I remember that as we walked through the fields, we saw other displaced families taking the same route as we did. Like us, they were fleeing the unknown present and the future to come. It was a humanistic movement for the preservation of the future of humanity—that's the way I saw it.

We had reached the point of looking for our last accommodation on this memorable trip. We were very excited and we talked nonstop about Wiesbaden-Biebrich, our hometown. We were in luck and found a clean barn at a nearby farm. It was clean, the farmer said, because it wasn't yet hay-making season. And we turned out to be quite lucky on this night because the roof was sound and we remained dry during the big thunderstorm that broke during the night. The next morning, we washed up with the hand pump in the barnyard, and we drank the water from the same pump. Mother made breakfast from the provisions we had with us, and we packed up and were on our way after thanking the farmer for the accommodations.

June 25, Day 12

This was the final day of our journey. We didn't have that far to go, but since the backroads were not the fastest way to travel, it still took the better part of the day to get to our destination. It was in the afternoon that we arrived at Grandma Trapp's apartment, at the Hammermuehle (in English, the Hammer Mill—it had been a mill where wheat and rye were ground). We had made such an arduous journey, but my grandmother was not happy to have four more kids, besides the twins, who were already living there. It turned out that there was no welcome wagon for us, and we stayed in the attic of the building for a few days.

Garden Shed Adventure

After that, we moved into our garden house, which was not very big and had a leaky roof. I remember one night in particular; as we slept, the rain came pouring in. It was a rude awakening to be drenched like that in the middle of the night. The garden was overgrown with berry bushes, and we had a wood-burning stove outside under a wooden trellis, which was also overgrown with wild berries. I remember that my brother Joseph had a birthday when we were still in the garden house, and the next door neighbors were American officers who had taken over the villa next door. The soldiers were friendly and liked my brother so they gave him a birthday party complete with ice cream.

The garden house wasn't weather-proof and so the situation had to change. Mother started looking for a place to live, but it wasn't easy. My twin sisters wanted to live with us, and that meant we were a family of six kids. It made it almost impossible to get a place. One day, she was in line at the Department of Housing and heard people talking about the former SS building on the river Rhine. The people in line said that the American military were occupying the place and there were signs that said it was off limits to unauthorized personnel and that no trespassing was permitted, but our mother had other responsibilities—six of them.

She went to check it out and it was not a pretty picture: the place was open, with people lying on the grass in the back of the building along the river. It was the summer of 1945 and nobody had jobs, so they just hung out by the water. There was no working toilet so the entire place was just as one big toilet.

A Bold Move into an Off-Limits Building

My mother decided to change all the locks and so she commissioned a local locksmith to do the work. Then she cleaned both floors of the building from top to bottom. (Years later, she told me that after all the cleaning, she lost her appetite and could not eat for a week.) This was around July 16th and we moved into our new place a few days after all the furniture was delivered. It was outside the city limits and we had to walk to school about two miles each way because in 1945 there were no streetcars in service.

The happy days were short lived, though. Three days after we moved in, we had a visit from four American officers. One spoke German and he translated. He told us to move out of the building as quickly as possible. It was under U.S. Command, they said. Mother replied, "I am happy to move if you get us a place to stay."

They inspected the place and asked who had cleaned it up. Mother spoke for a while longer and then they left. A week later, three of them came back and this time they were friendlier towards our mother. They explained why they had asked about the cleaning job—they needed a reliable person for their Club. So they offered her a job to be in charge of the club. She got paid and we could pick up food in their kitchen just like the soldiers. My mother got a job and we had a place to stay. Yes, that was the way with our mother: she stood her ground anywhere, anytime.

One thing I remember about the club—at night, people were always climbing in the windows looking for cigarette butts or anything else they could get their hands on. After those incidents, they hired a guard, and the problem was solved. One day, all of us were on high alert. My sister Liselotte, who was only five at the time, was nowhere to be found. We panicked and began searching the buildings, the grounds, and the river Rhine. After a while she turned up safe and sound sitting in a jeep—one of the soldiers had taken her for a ride. The soldiers were mostly young men and they missed their families very much, so we kids were sometimes the next best thing.

The Americans had their own water supply in the yard—a pool-like structure about twenty feet in diameter and four feet high made out of the heavy green tent fabric. At the time, they had to be sure the other side wouldn't poison the water supply. Even though it seemed like everything was nice and peaceful, some people were still not in favor of the Americans being in Germany.

At the end of 1945, the American military released the former SS-Marine-Storm-Boathouse to the City of Wiesbaden. A particular person was already interested in leasing the building. It was Heinrich Bachmann, who worked at the Rheinhuette factory across the street from the boathouse, where he was the head of personnel.

Wiesbaden-Biebrich, am Rheinufer

At the time, there were three boat clubs that didn't have a home, and the building was just the right space to provide those three clubs a home under one roof. So Heinrich Bachmann leased the building from the city of Wiesbaden in his name on the 8th of January 1946. By April 7, the first member meeting was held for all three clubs. And the new name was born: Wiesbadener Kanu Verein—WKV for short. In July of that year, the WKV received a license to operate as a canoe club. The lower part of the clubhouse was used as storage for the paddleboats, kayaks, and canoes. In July 1946, I was eight years old and was in charge of checking the members' passes to make sure that no one took out a boat without permission. It took me a while to remember all the members' names.

My twin sisters came to visit once in a while, but didn't stay very long because they had more privacy at Grandma's place. I recall one time in particular that my sister Ingeborg was taking care of us. Since our mother was not home, I climbed in the window to get a slice of bread, but Ingeborg caught me and she gave me a spanking I never forgot. She was only sixteen, but boy, was she strong! Times were still hard. You couldn't go to the store and just buy food. We still had food rationing, which meant you got food stamps for each person. It was not enough for living or dying.

So our mother went into the country to farmers to see if she could trade necessities such as toothpaste, toothbrushes, shoelaces, and shoe polish for bread. She had a knife to cut a slice of bread if she got some, but she never cut the bread before she came home. Many times she came home empty-handed.

On special occasions like regattas and other gatherings, my mother made her special iced tea that everybody loved. She used her copper washtub that was built into a wood-fired oven. The washtub was about twenty-two inches in diameter and about the same depth for brewing the tea. In those days, you couldn't get sodas or any other soft drinks since it was just after the war and before the new currency had come into circulation.

I remember the time my sister Liselotte and I walked barefoot to the beer distributor with a wooden wagon to pick up a case or two of beer. In those early years, we walked barefoot the whole summer. The roundtrip was about three miles and not too cool on your feet since the blacktop was hot from the sun beating down the whole day. Most of the time, we got the beer delivered. In the early days, they came with a pickup that had one wheel in the front and two in the back—it was called a three wheeler. There was another time we had to walk quite a distance. Mother got the word that grandma needed yeast to bake a cake. Since she did not get around too well any more, my sister Liselotte and I had to go and deliver the yeast. The trip was about two and a half miles each way. We started after school and got there in the late afternoon. The only thing was that by the time we got back, the yeast was almost gone. My sister got the taste for it and could not stop eating it. This was not a good thing. Grandma yelled at us and we had to go and get more yeast so she could bake her cake. It was in the fall so it got dark early and on our journey home we had to pass a cemetery. As we approached, we heard voices from the cemetery and we started running and screaming until we came to a well-lighted area. Yes, all those things happen to young people at times.

At this point, I lived for the WKV. I remember the first regatta at the Wiesbadener Kanu Verein in 1947. It was the first one after the war. I believe it was sometime in the beginning of 1948 that the members of the Club paid the total sum of 12,000.00 Reichsmark to purchase the clubhouse. The deal was made, another fine move from the top man, Mr. Heinrich Bachmann. Without him, the deal would have been impossible at the time. It was just before the new Deutsche Mark came into circulation. At one time in 1946 and 1947, we had refugees from the eastern side of Germany in the big ballroom, where portable partitions were installed for the privacy of the families. A deal was made between Mr. Bachmann and Dykerhoff Portland Cement Works, and these people were employed at the Cement Works. They stayed until Dykerhoff had space to place them in regular housing. After all the refugees were out, they could start with the important renovations. This was the same time that Kurt Seelbach, President of the Hessicher Kanu Verband, and his wife moved into the Boathouse, into the upper part just above us, the part with the dormer facing the Rhine River. In addition to running the restaurant part of the Boathouse for about seven years, my mother also kept the place clean. I remember the first New Year's party and the carnival parties to follow.

Those were special times indeed since the war was over and people were free to go where they wanted and enjoy their free time. And we kids went back to school. This was a time I have never forgotten since we lived in the suburbs of the city. The kids in school often started fights, and I would get my youngest sister Liselotte to help in the fight against the mob. I remember that my sister had a plastic pocketbook with a long strap. If she swung her pocket-book, that strap could really sting. Nobody wanted to get that sharp plastic edge in the face. That took care of most of the fights, although a few still went on. On my way home from school, I mostly met my friend Mr. Wilhelm Beck. At the time, he was the sole owner of the factory Rheinhuette. Wilhelm Beck was the brother of Ludwig August Theodor Beck, a general and chief of the German Army General Staff. Between 1935 and 1938, Beck became increasingly disillusioned in this respect, standing in opposition to the increasing authoritarianism of the Nazi regime and Hitler's aggressive foreign policy. It was due to public foreign policy disagreements with Hitler that Beck resigned as Chief of Staff in August 1938. From this point, Beck came to believe that Hitler could not be influenced for good, and that both Hitler and the Nazi Party needed to be removed from government. He became a major leader in the conspiracy to kill Hitler, and he would have been provisional head of state had the 20 July plot succeeded, but when the plot failed, Beck was arrested. Reportedly, he made an unsuccessful attempt at suicide, and was then shot dead. I often encountered Mr. Beck on my way home from school, at the Richard Wagner house and the Rheingau Strasse just across the street from his villa. He would remove his hat and greet me. I would tip my cap and return his greetings as we passed, and then we would each go home. At the time, he was living with his daughter and she would make lunch for him. Mr. Beck had a Mercedes and chauffeur, but he preferred to walk for his health.

In 1947, my sister Marianne came running home one afternoon all out of breath. She had seen two men hiding two twenty-liter canisters of gasoline in the bushes right across from our home at WKV. She dragged one of the tanks across the field and lawn all by herself and put it in our basement. My mother helped her put it into the wooden wagon, and they loaded the other canister. They took them to Rheinhuette for Heinrich Bachmann to deal with. Mr. Bachmann was the advisor in all those things post-war. A few weeks later, four guys visited our home at night and searched the whole house, including our living quarters. We kids were all in bed. These guys were from the Eastern Europe and did not speak English or German. After the search, they left and we never saw them again. Mother said there were looking for the missing gasoline.

1949 was a year full of surprises. The Deutsche Mark came into circulation and our father was released from the Russian prison of war. Finally, we children had a father to look up to. My father was a big and strong man. As prisoner of war, he had to install thousands of ceramic tiles in vodka stills. After his workday at the still, he would go back to the barracks. He always wore a heavy coat and under it, he would wrap a long hose around his body and fill it with vodka, which he shared with his comrades and the Russian security watchmen. The food was disgusting. They had nothing but frozen rotten vegetables. I spoke to some of his German comrades and they said, "If it had not been for your father's ingenuity—smuggling in the vodka and the other items he got through the post—we would have died."

Not very many guys were as talented as my father. At times, the officers would pay him to come to their homes to build a fireplace or tile a bathroom. He was paid in rubles and in food. Often, he went to the Bazaar (Market) and bought oranges, roasted chicken, French bread, and all things we never even knew existed at the time. The regular Russians were left out in the cold and it hasn't changed much since 1949. My father said that if he had been caught, he would have been put in solitary confinement.

There were times the officers were looking for my father to do some work. However, he was not to be found, as he had been put in a hole in the ground closed with a metal top and a full fifty-five-gallon barrel was placed on top for safekeeping. He was punished because he smuggled food in to the prison camp for his comrades and got caught by the wrong guard at the time. The guards were as poor as the prisoners of war. It wasn't easy to find the right balance between surviving and simply dying. My father said that there was only one way to survive—you had to take risks. Unless he took risks, he could not help his German comrades stay alive. Besides bringing in vodka and food, he was friendly with a nurse and the doctors, and did work

44

for the doctor and nurse to earn early release from prison. He walked through the bitter cold nights along the snow-filled railroad tracks to do the work, to save himself and his comrades. In return, the doctor wrote a report saying that most of the German prisoners of war in his camp had incurable illnesses. I recall one person telling me that, unlike my father, he had no work skills. He used to work at the employment office before the war. They were all glad just to be alive and they managed to get an early dismissal from DOS inhumane treatments. Most of those comrades overcame the hardship and went on to live happy and fulfilling lives with their families. I remember two boys who belonged to the WKV, and I believe their father was the man from the employment office.

Shortly after my father came back from Russia, in 1949, we leased from the city a piece of land on the Rhine that was on the street right next to the Kanu Verein. We planted tomatoes and my father built a chicken coop for our chickens. The tomatoes needed lots of water and in the evenings we kids carried bucket after bucket from the Rhine. Nearby, there was a metal factory. My mother spoke to the owner about some fence posts for our garden and we bought galvanized pipes and fenced in the garden. Mother asked the man how long those pipes would last and he replied, "Mrs. Lang, when both of us are long gone, the pipes will still be there." Last I checked, they've been in the ground for sixty years and they're still standing as a fence for the WKV.

I believe I learned how to swim in 1949. My older sister Marianne learned before me, as did my younger sister, Liselotte. I remember the boats with the big paddle wheels would come by and sometimes they created eight-feet-high swells. My sisters would just be swallowed up. My mother said her heart almost stopped when she saw those two out there swimming in the waves, and she would not let Liselotte swim without a life jacket.

The Kiosk Years

The following year was 1950. My father built a kiosk for our mother on our leased land next to the WKV and built new stairs out of concrete for the WKV. I remember I had to chisel the edges of the steps piece by piece so you wouldn't slip. First, he had to mason the two sides, and after we made the forms out of wood, poured concrete into the forms and made the stairs one at the time. After the concrete was set, we opened the form and I chiseled the edges. Since the steps were quite far apart, we had to roll the steps with a lever lift one side and then the other. My sister Marianne helped us move the steps and I remember that she got her finger under one of the rollers and screamed loudly. Our father didn't realize what had happened and told her to keep quiet so she wouldn't disturb everyone. After we finished the new stairs, we removed the last decayed wooden stairs on the left side of the building. My father was so talented he was able to do woodworking and masonry. He made all new doors for the lower part where the boats were kept and the work seemed never to end at the clubhouse.

We began with the men's bathrooms and the preparation was the biggest job. It was very dusty and all the walls had to be straightened and leveled. My father tiled the walls and the outside of the shower. I handed him the wooden matchsticks to use as spacers and we did all the work for material costs and very little labor.

In 1950, our mother started a kiosk. At first it was small—twelve feet by twelve feet. We sold candy, soda, and beer, mostly on weekends and in the summer. During the warm summer months, the business was good, and we closed over the winter months. I remember in the same year, we had young girls and boys visiting at the WKV from the Leverkusen water sport club. My mother acted as host and took care of the young girls. I remember that one of the young ladies was the daughter of the head of Bayer Aspirin. She asked my sister Liselotte and myself what toys we might like, and I asked for a puppet called Casper, a marionette. My sister asked for a queen puppet, and I recall the puppets arrived a few weeks later after the young lady's departure. I never got to thank her for the wonderful gifts, which gave us many hours of pleasure.

On some Sundays in the winter, I starred in the kiosks and charged an admission fee from the neighborhood kids. I made the stories up as I went along and the kids loved it. It gave us all entertainment. Of course, it was only possible in the winter when the kiosk was closed. In the back section was a wood stove that I fixed up to make it nice and warm for the kids. A Dutch door divided the front from the back and I used the lower part of it as a stage for my performance.

In the winter of 1949 to 1950, we sometimes went sleigh-riding. We only had sleds we made ourselves, but my sister's friend had a bobsled we all enjoyed. To get to the hills, we had to take a train and travel for about forty-five minutes. What I termed "hills" were actually streets that were closed for safety reasons. At the time, the city couldn't remove all the snow because there weren't enough trucks and other gear, so the kids could just enjoy it. I recall sometimes, Americans with their big cars drove uphill and pulled us along to the top, but most of the time we had to pull the bobsleds by ourselves. The reward came when we started the downhill journey. For lunch, we went to a nearby restaurant called Chausseehaus for a roll and some hot bouillon. I enjoyed the train ride home—wet, tired, and hungry after a full day. The restaurant and the train station, both called Chausseehaus, are still there.

In the 1950s, the summers were hot and we all had to help get ready for weekends at the kiosk. On Saturday and Sundays, people walked down the promenade, past our kiosk. The Coca-Cola, Pepsi, beer, water, and other soft drinks were delivered early in the morning—about thirty-five to forty cases of liquid—and it all had to be kept cold. So the iceman came and we placed the bottles into tin tubs. The ice came in large pieces—about 10x10 inches square and about forty-eight inches long—and we had to crush it with an icepick. After all the tin tubs were full, we placed a linen cloth over the whole tub. At the time, we had only limited electric refrigeration, so after working the whole day in the hot kiosk, sometimes there were no cold drinks left for us in the evenings. After we ended up with nothing left a few times, we planned ahead and made sure there was at least something cold for us to drink at night.

In the years to come, we expanded our business. My mother bought an ice cream machine and made homemade ice cream. This was a good move for those hot summer weekends, but she just made the ice cream so rich that there was no profit in the beginning. After a short time, she got the hang of it, the people loved it, and we made a profit too. In the coming months, we expanded again to become a delicatessen and sold breakfast to the workers of nearby companies. The butcher delivered fresh cold cuts every second day, and the bakery delivered fresh baked goods every morning. The business ran pretty smoothly but there were a few setbacks. One time, I recall a boy bought all kinds of candy and then took off without paying. I called out to my father who got on the bicycle and caught up with the boy a mile down the road. He happened to be the son of the neighboring town's mayor.

Another time, I was in the kiosk when two ladies came in to buy groceries. It was early in the morning, and they gave me a large bill as payment. Since it was early in the morning, I had no change. The one lady said she would go to the gas station and get some change. She took off with the bags of groceries. After a while, the second woman said she would go find her sister and she left too. She waved as if she had spotted her sister and disappeared around the corner. This was a professional con job. I left my post and went to look for them but they were gone.

I wanted to find out more about Thurn Castle and my cousin Ludwig Lang gave me information on the castle and its history, including names and dates. The seat of Thurn Castle is occupied by the royal family of Von Bentzel-Sturm Feder-Horneck. The castle was first occupied and taken over by the German military in 1943 to 1945. The quarters were used for patrol services and headed by Colonel Gruber and were also used as living quarters for people who had lost their homes in the bombing of Nuremberg and Furth. Many refugees found a safe haven at the castle. In 1945 to 1946, after the war, the American military made Thurn Castle one of their headquarters, so they could investigate various people and their connection to the N.S. Nazi party. They searched for war weapons, which they dismantled and submerged in the castle moat. After 1946, the royal family reclaimed their castle again, and has lived there ever since.

Today is Sunday, November 2, 2014 and the New York City marathon is under way. The wind is blowing forty-five miles an hour and I can't help but remember a day in 1946 when my sister Liselotte and I were home alone on a cold and nasty winter evening. The wind was blowing hard and the rain pounded against the house and the windows. Since the windows were single-glazed and opened to the inside, and the hardware was old and fragile, it didn't take long before they flew wide open. An eight-year-old child struggled mightily with the wind, but neither I nor my sister could overcome the force of the storm and the windows stayed open, as the rain and wind poured into the room.

We were up in the bedroom where we had a king-sized bed, so the best thing to do was hide under the bed for a while. Believe me, this was one experience I cannot easily forget, even though we were eventually rescued by one of our older siblings.

One hot summer day, I came home from school, did my homework, and was allowed to go out and play. Our home was surrounded on all sides by grass except in the front, which faced the Rhine. I don't know when my passion for horses began, but on that day there were about six horses on the side of the clubhouse lawn. I was so taken by them that I watched them all afternoon. As they kept up a light gallop, I sat on the grass and watched them with a passion. It got so late in the afternoon that I missed my supper. Finally, the horses went back to their stall on the outskirts of the city, and I followed the herd to their stall. It was late in the afternoon or early evening, and I remember I got home after dark and was surprised to find that no one was home.

It did not take long to find the rest of the family: they were down at the Rhine searching for me, terrified that I had been drowned. The day ended on a bittersweet note. I wasn't too happy with myself as I was a dreamer and sometimes got lost in time. The next day was such a happy one, though. We kids were surprised to learn that my sister Ingeborg was engaged to be married. What a happy time in our house. Yes, our sister was engaged to an American soldier, a lieutenant in the U.S. Air Force. A year later, they were married and they moved to the state of Georgia in the U.S.

One day in 1949, my mother got a good deal from her grocery salesperson: all the items she normally bought were greatly reduced, due to overstocking in the storage facility or warehouse, and my mother bought more than usual. The good fortune was short-lived, though, and the next day we found out that someone had broken into the kiosk and stolen all the goods. Since we had an alarm system on the windows at the kiosk and wooden shutters, there was no way in through the sides.

But we had overlooked a point of entry and in this case it was the roof, where we had no alarm. It was clear to us who the burglars were, but since we had no proof, we couldn't take them to court. The burglary put us in the hole for a while, but like anything else in life, another day came on the horizon. As the saying goes, let the clouds pass and the sun will shine on you again.

We kept a flower garden next to our kiosk. My brother Joseph was an apprentice to become a landscape gardener, so all the plants were well taken care of. And it was a joy to look at them the whole summer. He knew the Latin names for most of the plants. Roses were his specialty. He knew how to graft the roses and became a successful landscaper in his time.

Christmas with My Father in Bavaria

In December, as Christmas vacation was about to begin, our father asked us kids if we would like to come along for a trip to Bavaria. I believe I was the only one who wanted to go. I was eleven years old and I could hardly wait for the moment we would leave. Our journey began at night from the main train station in Wiesbaden. We went to Frankfurt and from there to Nuremburg, where we took a local train to Thurn Heroldsbach, arriving in the morning hours just in time for breakfast.

We made the night journey and arrived safely in Thurn Heroldsbach, which was just about fifteen minutes by foot to Grandma's house. This was my father's first visit to his hometown since he had returned from Russia, where he had been a prisoner of war. I could see the excitement on his face as we entered the town of Thurn, and he knew it was only 200 feet more to grandma's house.

In the distance, you could see a woman standing in her traditional black with a white dirndl, her arms raised and tears in her eyes. She called his name, "My Sepper, my Sepper," which means "Joseph." They held each other in a long loving embrace. My father was forty-three years old, and he had come back for the first time since the war, a war that had taken a lot out of everyone, kids and parents alike.

He was one of only three left out of a total of seven boys at the start of the war.

We stayed over the Christmas and New Year's holidays. There was lots of snow, and I went along to the forest to help cut pine trees. My father's brother Uncle Ludwig was living in the family home with his wife, Aunt Babert, and their two children, Renate and Margitte, Margitte was my favorite from those two girls.

My uncle Ludwig was a fine man and I liked him a lot as he was very generous towards me. Besides having his own painting business, he contracted on the railroad replacing damaged tracks. One time, a section of track was broken and all the help had to go help replace the track. The jobs had to be done right away no matter the time, day, or weather. One day, my father and I went to the next town with a big wooden wagon pulled by an ox. We had to bring a pig to another farmer for mating. On the way back, we had no load in the wagon and my father cracked the whip to get the ox moving. The ox started to run and my father could not stop him, as the gear came loose and there was no way to pull him back. In a panic, my father bent down to reach for the wagon brake, and in doing so he lost his balance and fell from the wagon. Now I was alone in the driver's seat and the ox kept running. It wasn't just the speed, but the gravel road was full of holes so the ride was very dangerous. I bounced from side to side with nothing to hold onto.

I looked back and saw off in the distance a man who I thought was my father, but the runaway wagon kept going with no end in sight. We galloped through forest and field on a ride of horror. It seemed like it would never end. After a while, the wagon came out of the woods and onto a road between the fields. In front of me, I saw a man in the distance running from the field into the middle of the road, and as we came closer, I realized that it was the farmer who had been working in the fields. He was standing in the middle of the road with his pickaxe held high in front of him, and the ox seemed to slow down until finally we came to a complete stop when we reached the farmer. I'm not entirely sure why we stopped. Maybe the ox was just tired.

It took a while for my father to show up and he was out of breath from walking such a distance. After he fixed the harness and checked the wagon for any damage, the journey continued. We were lucky there was no snow and the temperature was nice on this winter day. After a short ride, we came back home to grandma's place and had supper. I remember the sweet-sour taste of the bean soup. It was just so good.

At the back of Grandma's place was a pond that belonged to the local count von Bentzel-Sturm Feder-Horneck, who lived in the Thurn castle. He had several ponds in Thurn. My cousin Ludwig, who was ten at the time, had an air gun and we were target shooting from my grandma's back porch to the pond. These were memorable times: after our two-week stay, we had to leave, and the everyday chores at my house started all over.

My mother was not happy to hear the slang I had picked up while in Bavaria, and it took a while before I was able to lose it. I guess it's natural for a young person to want to blend in and be a part of his surroundings.

Remembering the Early Years

One day my mother, my sister Marianne, and my brother Josef went for a whole day in the forest to pick beechnuts. They then took them to be pressed into oil. My sister Liselotte and I were home alone for the whole day.

So I decided to make a swing. There were hooks on the ceiling beams under the open veranda at the WKV, our home at the time. We gathered some rope and a piece of wood for the seat. After the project was complete, I had my sister Liselotte try it out. Before I knew it, the rope tore away from the ceiling hooks and my sister fell face first onto the gravel floor. Her face was scraped and bleeding. So I decided to improve the swing and I tried it myself. The fun was short-lived, though. After a few swings, I too came crashing down.

I scraped my knees and legs and I was bleeding all over, crying and screaming. I ran to the nearby factory, Rheinhuette, where they had a first aid station, and they took care of me. My sister was the tougher of us two and didn't seek help. It was late in the evening when our mother and our two siblings returned from gathering beechnuts. We hid behind the door when they arrived because we were afraid we would get punished for what we had done. But everyone was happy that we only had minor injuries.

As I mentioned earlier, my sister Liselotte was called "Zwiebelschlotte," which rhymed with her name. Another of her nicknames was "Knottelchen," which meant that she was good with her hands and was able to fix things. I recall one time she was fixing the electrical cord from the radio. But she didn't test it herself, so she looked for a volunteer to plug it in. My sister Marianne was the one who volunteered for it, as we found out the project was successful.

My mother's birthday was coming up and my sister and I wanted to bake her a cake. We were around ten and eleven years old. Our kiosk was across the driveway from our living quarters at WKV. Since we had no recipe, my sister had to call over to my mother down at the kiosk by yelling across the driveway. To our surprise, the cake was a success. This started a new trend for my sister, the youngest of the family, who began to do the cooking. This was a big help for my mother because she was busy at her kiosk from morning to late evening.

Life continued to take its run into the 1950s and beyond. I was only twelve years old, and besides going to school, I helped at home with the everyday chores. We knew the water level of the Rhine was very high. The snow-melt at the higher elevations continued and the river kept rising. As soon as the Rhine crested its banks, we knew it was only a matter of time until the water reached the clubhouse.

I recall one day as I came home from school, the river was overflowing its banks and every hour, it came closer to our home. And you could see the water advancing by the minute. This meant we had to clean out our basement and move things to a higher elevation for safekeeping.

It took most of the afternoon for my brother and I to get all our goods in a safe place. But the real work was for the members of the club to take the paddleboats and kayaks that were stored on the lower levels and move them to the upper part of the building. All those boats had to be carried upstairs and stored on the veranda, and time was of the essence, since the water was advancing very rapidly.

This happened once or twice nearly every year depending on the climate change at the higher elevations and the melting process. We built a wooden bridge from our front patio to a higher area across the street. If the flooding occurred during the New Year's party, special care had to be taken with storing the boats so they were not in the way. One bit of adventure that I really enjoyed was when we could use our galvanized tin bathtub, which was stored in the basement, as a floating boat. One time when the water was about three feet high, we had to retrieve potatoes from a shelf in the basement, so the floating tub came in very handy. Of course, we had to tie it to the staircase so it wouldn't float away. When I think back, I realize that I had a pretty colorful life, but I didn't know it at the time.

The Owed Potatoes

I recall a time when I was about ten, my brother Josef was twelve, and my sister Liselotte was nine. My older sister Marianne was thirteen and she became friendly with two lady farmers who lived about ninety minutes by bus from our house in a town called Holzhausen a.d. Haide. The two ladies, Ella and Tilche, were sisters, and they ran a small farm which they had inherited from their family. Ella was the head of the family and worked the fields with a horse and plow. Tilche took care of the household chores, fed the animals, and kept the stalls clean. She also cooked all of our meals. It was late summer, and like all the farmers, the sisters needed extra help on the farm, so the three of us younger siblings stayed at the farm for the summer months to help out. We children accompanied Ella each morning to weed and plant the fields.

It was our summer vacation from school and we had to work. In lieu of wages, we were paid with potatoes, which we saved to live on during the winter months. While at the farm, we slept upstairs in the old farm house. We had a good-sized bedroom, but it was very dark with very low ceilings and very small windows to keep the heat in during the winter months.

At lunchtime, we would go back to the house to eat a fresh meal that Tilche had prepared. In those days, the hot

60

meal of the day was at lunch time, and most farmers had big meals of meat, potatoes and vegetables, which was new to us and we became rather spoiled. After our big lunch, we had to clean the stalls and the front yard, which was made of cobblestones and overrun by chickens and geese. We always had fresh eggs on hand, which where sold to a man who would take them to the city to sell. In back of the stall was a large garden with fruit trees and one large walnut tree. Sometimes, my sister Liselotte and I would go back there and collect a few walnuts. That ended the day my brother Josef told Ella, and we were scolded and told not to do that again.

The Lang Family 1951 Fritz and Liselotte confirmation

Life on the farm was different from our home life, as we were not used to getting up in the morning and going out to work in the fields. It took some adjusting for us, especially the last week of our stay. We had to harvest the potatoes from morning until dusk with only a short break for lunch. During harvest time, we did not go back to the house to eat lunch. Instead, lunch was served in the fields so as not to waste time going back and forth to the house. Back then, the farmers' homes and stalls were in town, and we had to travel back and forth to the fields by horse-drawn wagons.

In later years, I found out that my sister Marianne and her girlfriend Rosemary had worked at the farm the year before we kids started. But they were both about to turn fourteen and they preferred to make money instead of working for potatoes, so they got part-time jobs after school, which turned into full-time work in the summer.

After all the potatoes were in the barn and all the animals' winter feed was harvested and stored in the barn, we were free to leave. It was a hard job, but in those days, a child did not always have a choice if he was born into a certain living situation. In later years, the young people just walked off those types of jobs as they had more choices for work situations. However, I look back fondly at the farm work, as I considered it a great experience.

At the end of the summer, the three of us kids came home, and it was a change for both us kids and our mother. The school was a good fill-in for the long days. We never did receive our promised potatoes for which we worked, so we had to go out and buy our potatoes in the winter like everyone else. So as it turned out, the three of us were working for six weeks for food and shelter only.

Forty years later, I saw one of the sisters, Ella, walking through the town pushing a bicycle on which she was leaning heavily. As the story goes, Ella found a young doctor who promised to help her regain her youth, but in return he ended up with most of her money.

On another note, my mother divorced my father just about the time I was 13. It was not a pretty scene since my father would not leave by himself. We had to push him out of our home, as he claimed to have no place to go.

Father-Son Relationship

The next day I ran into my father on the street and found out to my surprise, he had a new permanent address. He moved in with one of his lady friends. Earlier this year he found employment in the factory, Rheinhuette, which produced pumps and pressure devices. The owner, Mr. Beck, was an acquaintance of mine. He got the job through our mutual friend Mr. Bachmann, who was the Personnel Manager of the factory responsible for hiring and firing. The foundry was in existence since well before the war and was in need of expansion. My father who was a Master Mason, knew all the ins and outs of the trade. He had many men working under him and it was not an easy job to watch all of them as well as follow the building plans and code. The buildings were all reinforced steel poured concrete. I found this out because in later years I was one of the workers. This factory like many others had their machinery all taken away by the American military and shipped to Russia by train where they sat and rusted completely and were never used again. I found out they confiscated only from the factories that made military items during the war. This was a process that always took place after a military takeover. Initially it was devastating but in the long run it was for the best. The German factories all got new machinery and a fresh start.

Yes, I was only 12 at the time and had to finish my schooling first before I could go out and earn some money on my own. Since we lived by the water I took a liking to water sports, but had no paddle boat of my own to enjoy it. One day a friend of ours came to the kiosk and was looking for a mason. He said he would like to build a two-family home for he and his son. I asked my father if he was interested in working on weekends to build our friend's house, since everyone worked regular jobs during the week. And my father said yes. When the job started I was the helper for the masonry. I remember the fine lunch the owner's wife and their daughter-in-law made. They went out of their way to make something different each week. At the time I was infatuated with the daughter- in-law, as she worked with us side by side helping with the cleanup and making mortar for my father's brick work. The entire basement walls were built out of a double layer of yellow bricks and stuccoed on the outside with a ½ inch smooth layer of cement which was then coated with two layers of liquid tar before they backfilled the foundation. After the foundation was completed the first floor was made out of reinforced concrete, and this was hard work since it had to be done by hand without any machinery. It was not too long before the rest of the work was done, since we just used concrete blocks and they were 8 inches high and 16 inches long. This speeded up the work tremendously. My job was to put mortar on top of the masonry with a shovel and my father then spread the mortar with the trowel and placed the concrete blocks on top.

This was the first money I made that would be used to purchase a used paddle boat. We worked every Saturday and Sunday during the summer and I came home tired every weekend. This was the first real job I had and it taught me discipline and respect for work. Yes, I could have stopped and stayed at home. However, I finished the job with my father and it felt very good. It was the first big money I made. It was about 400.00 DM (Deutsche Mark) which was equal to 100.00 U.S. dollars at the time. With this money I opened my first savings account which I was very proud of.

Christmas at Home

Christmas in the Lang home was a very special time. Our mother knew how to make the Christmas season an enjoyable and everlasting memorable event. On Christmas Eve she would decorate the six-foot-tall fir tree. Most of the time our mother decorated the tree by herself since we were still too young. It was a special privilege to be asked to be one of her helpers. She put the silver strings one at a time on each branch and selected the glass bulbs one by one for their color and size. And, not to forget, the white wax candles that were held by a metal clip candle holder.

The Christmas tree originated in Germany in the early years of Christianity, and came to England in 1840 during the ruling of George 3rd and his wife, the German born Queen, Charlotte. She would set up a candle lit fir tree in his palace at Christmas. And from there it spread to all the British Isles. The following years it came to North America and after that all over the Christian western world.

After we finished eating our dinner, we anxiously waited for the bell to ring. This was the signal for us kids that we could enter the room where the tree was. Yes, the excitement was in the air, but before we could open our presents we had to sing a few Christmas songs. In Germany you get your presents on Christmas Eve. Most of the time we had a good meal for the holidays. I remember on Christmas day we would have a goose with stuffing and all the trimmings. It was something to look forward to each year.

The hard times were in the past and you could buy almost anything in the stores for your DM. When my mother asked me for my Christmas wish I said I would like a presskopf, which is a piece of sausage that is cooked and processed pig meat formed in the shape of a ball. In the earlier years you could only dream of a wish like this to become a reality. I know it is a strange wish for a young boy, however, after the hard times we went through the only thing on my mind was food. My sister Liselotte, who was 10 at the time, wished for a doll and her wish also came true. The doll could open and close her eyes and say "mama". One remarkable thing about the doll is that it was not breakable. However, this was not the case. As our father was holding the doll he said "not breakable". He did not take into consideration his strength and hit the doll on the edge of the headboard from the bed and broke the doll's back in half. That was the end of my sister's doll, and none could replace it.

I am not sure if there was an attempt made on behalf of father to replace the doll, but one thing came out of it we knew not to let our personal items be inspected by our father.

Bavaria Around 1912

I n later years my mother recalled a typical dinner during her childhood. She told me between five of them they had one herring to share, and some potatoes. And, if they were lucky maybe some vegetables. My grandmother worked at the castle. At Christmas she said the local Baroness from the castle came to the less fortunate families and asked the kids what they wished for for Christmas. Sometimes they were invited to the Castle for hot chocolate and cookies.

As kids, they wished for ice skates and dolls. After they came home their mother asked what they wished for. She told them they should have asked for warm socks and underwear but the kids had different ideas. My mother said on Christmas Eve the Baroness brought toys and clothing for the kids. So it always was a warm and memorable time of year in the worst of times and the best of times.

Yes, no one could take away the family ties which held us together all these years and made us form a strong bond. And this was only possible by being honest and true to each other. My grandmother from my mother's side was married three times. I only knew my second and third grandmother's names. When my mother was born her last name was Eberlein. Her second and third married name was Trapp. The reason for the three marriages was during the first World War her husbands went missing or died. I remember the Trapp grandpa was a quiet guy and very nice towards us kids. I got my first used bicycle from grandpa Trapp and I painted it blue. That was my favorite color. It was something you don't easily forget.

My grandma raised four girls all by herself in a small country town called Oberzenn, Bavaria. My mother told me about a time when my grandmother delivered rolls and bread from the local bakery. This was one of many jobs she had. In the early morning hours she would walk to the next town which was about 2 miles each way, in any kind of weather, rain or snow, carrying a woven basket full of rolls and bread on her back. And on top of it she placed her 10 month old baby, which was my mother. She didn't realize it at the time, but, the baby made all the basket goods wet during the journey. It was not a pretty sight since the diapers where made from cotton fabric and did not hold the liquid well. I found out later the baker liked my grandma so she didn't lose her job.

The Soapbox Derby

In 1949 there was a soapbox derby put on by the American military at the USAG Wiesbaden Herald Union. At the time it was widely advertised throughout the city so I got a good look at one of the posters. I could not walk away without getting hooked. There was more to it than meets the eye: you had to go to meetings and then finally you got a sponsor for the wheels. The ball bearing wheels and axle were made by the Opel Car Manufacture Company (a sister company of GMC). My sponsor was the Baba brewery, a beer brewery of Bavaria. Their local distributor, which was located in the city of Wiesbaden-Biebrich, about 15 minutes away from the boats builders place by car, supplied the wheels for me. The main reason I entered the soap box derby was that whoever won first place in Wiesbaden advanced to the final race and the winner of the final got to go to America.

After I got my wheels I had to start on the soapbox. I was friends with a local boats builder, Franz Dinewitzer, and could build my soapbox at his shop. I spent all my free time at his workshop for years. I recall one day when I brought a brown bag lunch from home, I tried to pick it up but could not move it. After close inspection I found it was nailed to the workbench. This and other pranks made the day go by with a smile. Another time there was a lot of

71

wood chips from the wood planer and Franz had a hole in the floor covered with a lid. After I had filled the hole I had to go down and distribute the wood chips. It didn't take long, but while I was down there he closed the lid on me and put a heavy weight on top. Since I knew the routine from before I wasn't too upset; I rested a while and in good time they let me out. Franz, the master boats builder, cut all the wood on the heavy machinery and I assembled the soapbox.

I got the soapbox ready in time for the race in Wiesbaden. It was painted blue with a white base and the brewery logo on it. I was very excited for the race. It was a hot summer day and my 2 Sisters, Marianne and Liselotte, and my brother, Josef, were there. I was winning the first race and had to wait till the afternoon for the second chance to get going In the meantime, Marianne and Josef left. I believe it was only Liselotte who stayed around. Finally, the second race started and I was first at the beginning but came in second at the finish line. The winner was the soapbox sponsored by Coca–Cola company. The streamlined body was molded and had a highly polished finish in red with white writing. It was a dream machine that no 10-year-old boy could ever build. If you had the right connections you had it made. It was a whole day affair since I had to stay until the end because all participants received a reward, a certificate of participation in the race, and your rank. I got so many other things too—Coca-Cola, potato chips, and boxes of chocolate and candy. My soapbox car was full and the journey home was 6 kilometers long. I had to push the car because there was no one who could put the soapbox on a truck or drive me home unlike in the morning when the brewery picked me and my soap box up and drove me to the racing destination.

This was another chapter in my life which I remember dearly, especially since we didn't have a lot of money. There was always hope for the better.

The Missing Chocolate Bars

It was a few weeks before Christmas. Our mother had gotten a good deal on some chocolate bars which she safely tucked away. At the time you could not get chocolate in any store, only on the black market as they called it. She had gotten chocolate bars for each of us by trading some tobacco for chocolate. The tobacco came from the American soldier's night club. Our mother took care of the place and cleaned the club so there were all the cigarette butts you needed. Yes, times where still hard for most people in 1945 and '46, especially for a woman with 6 kids to provide for. At the time we had our cousin Kathy staying at our house because her mother, our aunt, was ill at the time.

Now it was a few days before Christmas and our mother looked for the hidden chocolate bars. To her surprise all of the chocolate bars where gone and there was no trace of them anywhere. After questioning all of us kids about the disappearance of the bars none of us claimed to have taken them. I came to the conclusion that our cousin Kathy, who was the oldest, must have found them and eaten them. Our mother told us since the beginning of time that stealing and lying is the worst thing you can do. I know there are worse things in life but for us it was a bad thing to lie or steal. My sister Inga's sister-in-law, Audrey, and her husband, Harold, who was stationed at the time in Weisbaden, heard about the missing chocolate and purchased, in the military store, a box of Hershey's chocolate. We were overtaken with joy to see so much chocolate.

So, the mystery will never be revealed. However life goes on and bigger mysteries go unsolved. It's hard to believe that after sixty five years we still talk about the missing chocolate and the surprise gift of the box of Hershey's once in a while, and wonder what ever happened to those chocolate bars. I guess it will stay a mystery forever.

The Apprenticeship Years

It was in the late spring of 1953, just before my fifteenth birthday. My mother and I traveled by streetcar to the next town in search of an apprenticeship position for me at a cabinetmaker's shop. We had seen an ad in the daily newspaper for a job in a town called Amoeneburg, so we got off the streetcar when it stopped there. My mother took me to a nearby snack bar, and she got a bouillon with a raw egg in it for me to give me strength and energy. After the power drink, we had a ten-minute walk to the woodworking shop. The boss, Mr. Ziob, was in and we negotiated terms of a three-year apprenticeship. The first of the three years I was to receive 25 marks per month, which was equal to $6.25 at the time. Each following year, I would receive an increase of 10 marks. The shop was in a big compound—a former military facility. The buildings were made to last many years: concrete blocks of stucco with sandstone and a slate roof. The apprenticeship started in the fall of 1953, after my fifteenth birthday and the summer school break, and it was a big change for me. I had to start at 7:00 a.m., rain or shine, so I had to leave my house at 6:15 a.m. to allow for the thirty-minute bike ride from my home. This meant I had to keep my bike in top shape at all times, especially in the winter months, as it got dark early, and the lights on the bike had to be in good working order.

I recall one night after work, it was just about twilight and I was biking home when my lights stopped working. As I rode along a straight stretch of road, I saw the police pulling cars over to the side, one after the other. After seeing this, I turned around and bicycled back as fast as I could. As I glanced behind me, I saw a police car following me. I pedaled away as fast as I could, my heart beating heavily and sweat running down my shirt. When I reached the house of my friend, Klaus, which was across from work, I hid behind their house. To my surprise, the police passed by the house, so after a while I continued on my journey home. I remember these trips to work very well because in those days there were no bicycle paths, and one had to share the road with the regular traffic.

The job was a big change from doing school work and chores at home. It was not easy being in a place where you had to work from morning to evening. I was one of three apprentices. One boy, Peter, was in his second year, and the other, Klaus Weilacher, was starting with me. For some reason I did not understand, the other journeymen in the shop did not like Peter.

Klaus and I, the newcomers, had to start the glue oven and the potbelly stove. The glue oven had a surface of 4x8 feet, and on one side there was an attachment to hold three pots of glue, which contained pearls of glue to which water was added to make hot glue. On the top, we heated the tin metal sheets for the hand press. Since the glue cooled off before all the wood was placed in the press, the hot tin metal sheets gave the glue a second warmup before they were molded in the press to the shape we wanted. The pot-belly stove was about eighteen inches in diameter and forty-eight inches high. To heat the stove, you had to put a steel pipe in the middle—about three inches in diameter—and pack the remainder with wood shavings and sawdust, and you had to pack it solid. After all this was done, the pipe was pulled out and the fire was lit. In the middle of the stove was an air shaft, which was created by a steel pipe. The stove heated the area of the woodshop where the work benches were located, and the heat lasted almost the whole day.

Before leaving the shop at night, we had to prepare all the stoves and clean up the sawdust and wood shavings. The first year of the apprenticeship, we had to do all the helpers' work. The only break we got was on Wednesday, which was a school day, so we got to catch our breath. Our teacher was cool. His name was Ficke, which in English means "fuck." The first day at school when he introduced himself, the whole class roared with laughter, but he was proud of his name and would not change it for anything. The school lunch break was an hour, during which time Klaus and I and sometimes some friends walked around the city, and we enjoyed our freedom. It was only a short-lived freedom, but it was better than nothing, and we could go back to the job recharged.

The first year was an adjustment year, and we had to get used to the language and manners different from the ones we were accustomed to at home. Most of the workers were a bit on the shady side, but not everyone in the wood-shop was bad. We had an experienced cabinetmaker, Anton Kling, and he was a master of his trade. If time allowed, he showed us the different ways to prepare and work with all types of wood. Sometimes we made elegant kitchen or bedroom cabinets with inlay veneer, and all this was made from scratch, meaning we did not use any finished plywood, only our own. Those were the days when you could order anything, and we made it from scratch. We made big sheets of plywood and joiner sheets, which meant that we cut the wood in strips five-eigths of an inch and applied two layers of veneer on each side. The first layer was cut across and was not the best cut. The outer layer was the finished layer and that was sometimes specially done with an inlay picture.

Our boss received a lot of contracts from the American military for wooden screen frames for the upper military ranks. The military men lived in the villas in all the confiscated homes, so our woodshop was turning out wood frames with no end in sight. After all the wood was cut and made into frames, Klaus and I had to paint them and later install aluminum screen wire. After the screen wire was applied, we finished the top with the final wood strip and gave it another coat of paint. Later, we installed the frames. I went along most of the time with our top man, Mr. Kling. We only had a three-wheeler pickup so we had to be very careful that it didn't turn over, especially when going around sharp corners. There was a large frame in the middle of the loading platform on which to fasten the oversized screens so they would not get damaged during transportation. We often had to drive for a long time to get to our destination. It turned out that the frames did not fit well because the boss man did the measurements, but we had to make things work, so we installed the frames as well as we could. I enjoyed the installation part a lot as it was a nice change for us boys to get out of the shop and into the fresh air.

As the second year of the apprenticeship approached, we made more furniture, especially in the winter months. I recall one of our bigger jobs when the contract was for us to completely furnish and install the new military pharmacy for the largest American military hospital in Europe. It was called Camp Pierre, a large compound on the outskirts of the city of Wiesbaden.

The building was one of many former German military facilities. It was furnished with a new heating system, and the heat came from a nearby furnace facility where it was pumped into all of the surrounding buildings. Our company's job was to install a wood floor over the existing vinyl tile-covered concrete floor. After the floor was installed and the electrician's work completed, the new windows were installed. It was then ready for our cabinets to be installed. First, the large shelving arrived and was installed from the floor to the ceiling between the windows and around the door frames. It started with a twelve-inch base and went all the way up to the ceiling, which was about nine-feet high. To reach the top, we installed a rolling ladder to go all around the room.

The material was birch plywood, custom made in our woodshop. All the counter cabinets, of which there were many, were installed in the following weeks. While I was working at the facility, I noticed a man in his forties follow-ing me every time I went into the courtyard to get some-thing out of our utility truck. I was sixteen at the time and did not know what to make of it. After I spoke to the top man, Mr. Kling, he smiled and said the man was gay and was looking for a young companion, so I knew to watch out for him. I was anxious to get out of that kind of situation; I didn't need the piercing eyes of this guy following me all around. I looked forward to completing the job. It took a while to get that out of my mind and go about my normal life.

It was the spring of 1956, and the final year of the apprenticeship was approaching. The woodshop was still going strong and we made more screen frames than ever. One rainy Monday morning, we left the woodshop with the three-wheeler pickup heavily loaded with cargo in the back. We had to drive with caution on the wet cobblestone pavement. Later in the morning, the sun came out and we worked on the screen installation. It was just before lunch as we finished a job at a villa outside the city of Erbenheim when the foreman asked me to bring in the paint pot to give the wooden screen frame a final touchup so we could move on to our next destination. As usual, I ran to get the paint. I didn't realize that the lid was not closed tight, and I tripped over the thick Persian carpet in the dining room and spilled the entire can of white oil paint on the carpet. We spent a long time trying to clean up the paint, and we never got it all out.

It was one of those days when no matter how hard you try, nothing seems to go right. After we exhausted all of our know-how, the final result was a disaster. We left for our next job and left the mess for our boss to work out. When we returned to the woodshop, it was my responsibility to report the incident to the big boss. It was never easy to report bad news, but to my surprise, the boss took it well. As I recall, there was no screaming or yelling, but in the coming weeks I was informed that it was a very expensive rug and the insurance company had to replace it.

Another experience I remember well was when we had a job rebuilding an old movie theater. It was an all-hands-on-deck job: all of us, young or old, had to be there from morning to evening. The teardown was a messy, dusty job, and no one wore a mask or any other protection. In those days, you either worked or stayed at home, so no one complained. After the war, people needed to replace what had been lost, so no one could be choosy about their job or their salary.

The Teen Years and Beyond

I n the 1950s, one could earn more working at a construction site than laboring in a wood-working shop, so during those years I worked side by side with my father and earned a good salary. In order to sell beer at the construction site, I made myself a cold box lined with tin and got ice from our store to keep the beer nice and cold. On a good day, I sold about forty 18 oz. bottles of beer. The beer box had a padlock to keep the beer secure.

One day after working in the woods, I went to the shack where the beer was kept. Someone had broken the padlock on the beer box, and I could see the hammer markings on the box. I estimated the damage when payday came, and I locked everyone in the shack and no one left the shack that day until the damage was paid in full. Those sorts of things happened on all construction sites—luckily for me, it never happened again.

At WKV, I became a member of the canoe club and joined the kayak racing team. I had some money in the bank from the year before when I had worked with my father on weekends building a house for a friend. After looking carefully for a used paddleboat, I found a one-seat boat. The bottom and the sides were made of a silver rubber-like material and the top was blue canvas. We called it a foldboat because it could be folded up and stored in two canvas bags. The hull fit in one bag, and the wooden ribs, which fit together with brass sleeves, in another. These were the specifications for the foldboat as I remember them: The ribs were spindled about half an inch in diameter and came in different lengths, between twenty-four and thirty inches, and the frames were made of ash wood.

I made some new friends at the canoe club. It meant a lot to me to be accepted by the other boys my age. I had met most of the boys from having brought bicycles to the club the previous year. One boy, whose name was Karl Heinz Deeg, but who was called Sam by his friends, was our neighbor across the street from the club. Another friend was Hans H. Deucker, whose friends called him Heine. Werner Hinter was another of the pack and he was called Strich, which meant "line" in English, or they called him Herring because he was so skinny. The oldest and the leader of the pack was Friedrich Dielmann, who we called Emmes, and his younger brother Heinz, who was called Marshal. As my friendship with the boys grew, big lifestyle changes started happening for me.

One of the first changes was going out and drinking with the boys, and trying to drink as much or more beer than they did during the course of a hot summer afternoon. I was not a pretty sight after all that drinking. We would consume so much alcohol on these afternoons that the next day we felt like we were dying, and we all made slow recoveries. Another activity that was a change for me was when I accompanied the boys when they went camping on the weekends. We took our paddleboats, tents, and any gear we needed for the weekend and headed up river to a campground called Goldgrund, where WKV members were allowed to camp. Because we all worked until late before the weekend, it was often too late to paddle all the way to the campground. Because we did not like to paddle in the dark of the night, we went to the other side of the Rhine River and let the big freighter pull us upstream. It was not an easy thing to do since the ships were moving and we were there with seven boats at the same time. First, we would befriend the captain of the ship. We would wave a bottle of beer and one would wave okay, and each boat, one by one, got hooked up to a rowboat. Each of the freighters pulled a rowboat with a heavy rope for safety reasons. In the event of a fire, the crew could escape to safety in the rowboat. The journey took about an hour from start to finish. At the end, we gave the captain of the ship the beer we had promised him.

As we got close to the campground, we paddled the rest of the way. You couldn't say we didn't have endurance. Getting back to the freighter, or tugboat, as it was called, they pulled about eight to twelve barge-like motorless boats behind them that were about 3 kilometers in total length. Since the freighters were connected with steel cables between the ships, we had to be very careful, because if the cable tightened, our paddleboat could snap in half. It goes without saying that teenagers take dangerous risks, and these weekends spent with my new friends were always enjoyable.

There was a very strict dress code at the WKV. On Sundays we had to wear a suit and tie to get into the clubhouse. Once we got there, we changed into club shorts or jogging pants depending on the time of the year. If it was a warm summer day, we wore the club color shorts—blue with orange stripes. The tops were the same material and color. It was not hard for me to dress since I lived at the clubhouse. So once I put on my shorts and t-shirt, I was ready for the boat trip to a sand bank across the Rhine River. This is where the young people were swimming at the beach across from the clubhouse on an island called Rettbergsau.

Sometimes on the weekends, I would go to a job site which was just five minutes away from the clubhouse to spray water on the concrete. Since I was the youngest and lived the closest to the job site, I was chosen to pour water on the fresh concrete so it wouldn't dry too fast and crack. The concrete was covered with cloth canvas to keep the ultraviolet rays from penetrating it. After watering the cloth, the concrete could stay wet longer. So on the occasional Sunday, this was my job, and I did not mind a bit because I could still go across the Rhine and bathe at the sand beach and be with my friends. I would make the trip across the Rhine a few times on hot summer days to keep the concrete wet.

I recall that on one of those Sundays, I met a very nice young lady at the beach at the Rettbergsaue. She was about my age and was there with her younger brother. One day, we walked all the way to the end of the island and swam downstream to the beach—about one and a half mile stretch. One late afternoon, I took her and her brother, one at a time across the Rhine in my boat. They changed into their street clothes at the club and we had food and drinks. She and I made a date to meet again, and we went to the movies, but the chemistry wasn't right between us, so it was a short-lived romance. Those brief romances happened quite often—sometimes the one you like is just not in the cards for you. I realized later in life that things would not have worked out since our lives were far apart.

It was not an easy job working for my father at the construction site. Some days we poured concrete into the wooden form of a pillar that was about twenty feet high. We had to climb a ladder to get to the top to fill the pillar with the concrete. You hauled up a container on your shoulder. It was open in the front and had a handle below the opening to hold it in place. This container was about three feet long and ten inches high, and the bottom was eight inches and the top ten inches wide. After you reached the top of the ladder, you had to bend forward and pour the eighty to one hundred pounds of concrete into the twenty-foot pillar. This was a slow process and by the end of a day, we were exhausted. The good thing was that we only had to do this job once a week, after all the steel was bent and put in place (the pillar was a skeleton of steel enclosed by wooden forms). The concrete floors were mostly poured on the weekends, so the cement mixer ran nonstop on Fridays from morning until we left in the afternoon.

Our WKV team, or group, as it was called, was unique in that we were all there for each other. I recall one occasion when Emmes noticed that some of his money had gone missing. After a meeting with the group, we suspected one person and decided to set up a sting. We called the suspect, an electrician who occasionally worked at the clubhouse, and told him that the light in the locker room was not working. We placed a wallet with money in the pants pocket in the room and hid. Sure enough, the electrician showed up and took the money. Then later in the evening, after most of the members of the club had left, we placed another call to the suspect and claimed there was no electricity in the main ballroom. It took a while for the electrician to come, as we hid in the dark. Once he got there, we confronted him and he screamed out of fear, afraid that we would beat him up. Soon, though, Mr. Kurt Seelbach came to his rescue. He lived upstairs at the time and always told us not to take the law into our own hands. The thief then paid the money back and we never had a problem like that again.

After this incident, the electrician no longer worked in the WKV and was banned from entering the clubhouse. The team of six of us did a lot of work around the clubhouse: keeping the grounds clean, cutting the grass, and making sure the float was fastened properly during the boating season. In the late fall, we took the float out and stored it on the lawn during the winter months.

Girls in Distress

One Sunday morning in the late 1950s, I prepared my one-seat foldboat for a ride. I got ready before the members got there and paddled around the island called Rettbergsau, which was just across from our clubhouse. I went upstream to the tip of the island, went around it and headed back downstream. As I came to the end of the island, I entered another township called Schierstein. There was a harbor there where all kinds of boats were docked, and there were lots of people who had come to swim, as the local beach was open. Many people had arrived in boats from all different townships to spend the hot summer day on the beach.

As I came around the island, I heard women screaming. When I checked out what it was, I saw two young ladies floating on their motorboat, and it looked like their motor had stopped working. They were drifting towards a rock formation. They yelled in terror for help, and seeing no one else around, I steered my boat towards them and fastened a line from my foldboat to their motorboat. I paddled as hard as I could and after a while I managed to get the boat away from the rocks. I then paddled upstream with the motor boat in tow. After struggling for a while, I finally got the motor boat fastened up to a nearby dock.

The young ladies called me their lifesaver. I stayed with them until we got more help from the harbor where they kept their boat. As we waited for the mechanic from their boat yard, it was nearly lunchtime. After about an hour, a big motorboat arrived with the owner of the boat-yard, his wife, a friend, and the friend's daughter who was about my age. Although I was free to leave at that point, they persuaded me to stay and have lunch with them. After some minor repairs were made to the boat, they took me in tow, and we went to the end of the island where it was quiet and peaceful. There was not much of a current, and we tied our boats to the overhanging tree branches. We ate lunch there and drank some beer and hard liquor.

It turned out to be a day full of surprises. The young girl's name was Simone, and we went swimming together. She was close to my age and we spoke the same language, as young people do. We had lots of fun together, and it didn't take long for me to fall head over heels in love with her. That day all of us had drank a lot, and a few hours later, when the alcohol was wearing off, everyone went on their way. I paddled home, knowing that I was expected to be all dressed and ready to go out later to Wiesbaden with my newfound girlfriend, Simone, and her mother.

After I got ready, Simone and her mother picked me up in their Mercedes Benz and we went to the city of Wiesbaden. They had a very large apartment decorated with antique furniture. Simone's mother was an actress who appeared in many German movies, although none that I had seen. At the time, pizza was the new fad in foods, so they ordered it. As I recall, it was not my kind of food. As the evening continued, they told me that Simone's father was a president of a big company and he was away a lot. They had a lot of material things but not much of a family life, as her mother was on the set making movies most of the time and her father was away at the company. So Simone was left alone at an early age, and her grandmother took care of her. I had to go home that evening because the next day was a workday, Monday. I saw Simone a few more times, but eventually we drifted apart because she was in school and she lived out of town.

I had gotten a look into the lives of the rich and famous, and all I can say is that it wasn't as glamorous as it looks from the outside. Not everybody can handle this situation without help from a psychiatrist. I must say from my own experience that a good family life is like money in the bank. As I continued through life, I always cherished my family's open and honest discussions. Those are the riches you can ask for in hopes they are there for you.

Family News

When I came home from work, my mother was still working in her kiosk. It was the fall of 1956, and the big news was that my sister, Marianne, was engaged to be married to Lothar Seifert. They planned to live in a town called Holzhausen a.d. Haide. In 1956, it was about one hour by car from Wiesbaden-Biebrich, although today you can make it in about thirty-five minutes with the new and improved roads. Holzhausen is a medium-sized township, consisting at the time of mostly farmers, both small and large. The Seifert's were small farmers and had eight cows and the town bull. If a farmer in town needed to mate a cow, they came to the Seifert's, and the mating was done right there in front of the stall. They also had a dozen chickens and six pigs across the road in a stall next to the barn. There was a small garden next to the house where they planted flowers and vegetables.

My sister Marianne was very athletic, and as I recall, she wanted to be a gym teacher. She was always boating or swimming and wasn't into household chores or cooking. She worked at a place called Henkel where they made sparkling wine, which is called *Sekt* in German. I remember the Henkel building had a Red Cross painted on the roof, and it remained undamaged during the war.

On another note, Mother got a letter from the City of Wiesbaden informing her of when she could move the kiosk from its present spot. Since we were no longer caretakers of the canoe club and only occupied the apartment, there was time to move from the clubhouse to the new quarters. This had been in the works for a while but without any result until this time. After mother consulted with Mr. Bachmann about the situation, it was decided that both parties could benefit. Since the German government had never reimbursed us for the house that was destroyed during the war in 1944, we were offered an empty building lot one city block south of our kiosk that we could purchase for the same amount we had sold our building lot for in the Gibb. So it looked like we were getting a new start twelve years after the war. Mr. Koehler, who worked in the department for land situated on the Rhine, was the one who made it possible for us to get that piece of land. Mother knew him and he used to come to the kiosk. It was my sister, Liselotte, who bicycled across the Rhine Bridge to the city of Mainz to pay for the land. At the time, no chores were too big for us kids.

We had our hands full with the new project. The building lot was located on Regattastrasse, just about a two-minute walk from the clubhouse or our nearby kiosk. After all the paperwork for the sale was completed, we had to get a building permit. The property was in a flood zone, so we had to fill in the building lot one and a half meters (approximately five feet) to get it out of the flood zone. Since the company I was working for excavated new buildings, we could get all the fill we needed. We then had to put up a reinforced concrete wall faced with stone to hold the five feet of dirt in place. It was a long drawn-out project since we had to do all the labor ourselves—that is, my brother Joseph and I had to do it. After we got the building permit and started filling in the lot, the fill had to be spread out evenly by hand. The first year, we put down grass seed to hold the dirt in place. We then had to look for an architect for the house design since we could not put our kiosk on the property. We had the architect include a store in the design and that turned out to be a better deal, because our home and delicatessen were in one building. The plan was approved by the building department and we began digging the basement. It was 1958 when we started building the project, and it took almost two years from the first discussion about it.

Easter Trip

At Easter, my friends and I paddled down the Rhine to where it merges with the Lahn River, and from there we paddled upstream on the Lahn. The journey took four days. In Germany, the Friday before Easter and the Monday after it are holidays. The first day, Friday, we started out in the late morning, and the first stop was St. Goarshausen, where we arrived in the afternoon. It was not warm enough for camping outside so we made arrangements to sleep on the floor of the restaurant on our air mattresses and sleeping bags. Most bars in those days had a built-in bowling lane, so we could set up our mattresses there after closing time.

It was our first night sleeping away from home for the season and it felt good to be away on tour. It was a treat to be with boys my own age. After we had a good breakfast, we got in our boats and continued our journey from the Rhine down to the river Lahn. On our trip, we passed a lot of big passenger boats. I felt sorry for the people in their suits, all dressed up on the upper deck. We were dressed in casual summer sportswear and were drinking cool beers. Our beer was always cool since we kept it tethered to the boat about eight feet underwater. As soon as we came close to running out of beer, two guys headed towards the next town and got a new supply.

The Rhine has the most beautiful countryside and the best scenic sites, starting from the more than 2000-year-old city of Mainz to the world famous city of Cologne. There are wonderful mountainside castles and well-groomed vineyards, and below that are small towns best known for their fine wines. The Rhine has many bridges, and the small towns can only be reached by ferry, which adds another romantic side to the city.

The Rhine is fed from about three different springs at its origin in Switzerland and it flows through Lake Constance, and from there northeastward into the mouth of the Rhine. Many smaller rivers feed the Rhine all the way to its endpoint in Holland, where it spills into the Dutch three-armed delta to the North Sea.

After lunch, we came to the outlet of the Lahn at the town of Lahnstein and went upstream on the Lahn. This meant we had to paddle for a change, and we loved that because it got us ready for the night life. At our next stop, we would spend the night in the town of Dausenau. It was unexpected scenery and quite unexpected to be going through and over the locks. From Dausenau to our destination, we had to overcome four locks in total. I had never seen locks before, so I was fascinated by how those worked.

Not all the locks were working so we had to take our boats and carry them around to the higher elevation. As it got too late in the day, the lock operator had left. The place where we stayed was a sports center right at the water's edge, so we did not have far to go with our bags. After we all settled down and got washed up, we were ready to paint the town red. First we had to find a good place to eat. We looked for a butcher with a restaurant since the portions there were usually bigger. After a good healthy meal, we were ready to have fun. We started at a place with music to get us in the mood to dance with the local girls. It was kind of risky since the local boys were not fond of strangers. If danger arose, we had a backup weapon—a baseball bat Emmes had been given when he was boxing at the American military. His brother-in-law was an American soldier and he had gotten him a job boxing at the military base.

Most of the time, the parties went smoothly, but the next day I usually had a headache. I remember one night I met a young lady that evening and there was a lot of dancing and smooching going on, and a lot of alcohol to facilitate it. I remember the guys told me the girl was looking for me in the morning. They lifted me up and tried to carry me back to see the girl, but we didn't have time as we had to go on with our trip to the next lock, which was called the Dausenau Lock.

I was the one chosen to go see the man working in the tower. After I spoke to the man in charge, I walked back and looked down and saw my friends yelling that they were opening the lock. At the time, I had no experience with locks and was not thinking about what could happen. I did the next best thing and took one leap towards my boat off an eight-foot wall. To the amazement of everyone watching, including myself, I landed in my boat. I think this was a fluke and I'm sure I could never do that again. I didn't have a scratch on me, which was amazing because the opening of the boat was only about eighteen inches wide and thirty inches long and it came to a point in the front. Will wonders never cease? After this experience, we had a new topic of conversation for a while and the journey continued through five more locks. Our next destination was Balduinstein, just before Diez, where they have the Waterways and Shipping Administration. It was day number three, and we found another good eating place with entertainment. We had another boys' night out with lots of laughs. We got to bed early that night, and the next day was the last day of the trip. We had to overcome just two more locks before we got to a city called Limburg. After lunch, we took our boats apart and put them in bags, and our bus picked us up in the early afternoon for the trip home.

Job Change

I t was after the Easter holidays when I decided to change job locations. After two years working as a construction helper at my father's job site, I felt it was time to work in the trade for which I was trained: the woodworking shop. I applied for a position as a cabinetmaker in the same factory, Rheinhuete, and was accepted. Now I had more leisure time for myself, my friends, and family. It came to my attention from a friend at the canoe club that they were looking for people to act in the States Theater. There was a part for a soldier in the Italian play, "Aida" by Verdi. I had always had an interest in the performing arts and entertainment so I was all ears. This was my chance to mingle with the stars.

It was the highlight of the season when I worked as an extra at the States Theater. I volunteered any chance I got to be on or behind the stage. The performing arts was my new hobby, and I could not get enough of it, although it was only seasonal. One night on my way home from the theater, I stopped at a local pub for a drink. After I left, I realized there were three guys following me, and they were talking loud enough so I could hear them. They were saying that they were going to get me, and there was no one around to come to my rescue. The streets were empty and it was pretty dark. I had to make a quick decision on how to get out of this mess. I came to a small side street where I stopped and turned around with my right hand on my upper chest under my topcoat and pulled slightly back. I called to the guys to come over, and when they saw me, they ran and screamed, thinking that I had a pistol. They ran like lightning, and soon there was no trace of them. So now the tables were turned and I could go home peacefully. As my father once said, these things happen in life and you have to know how to get out of them on your own. I often found myself in tight situations that I had to get out of without getting hurt.

The new job was very nice. I was in charge of the glass for the whole factory. As soon as there was a broken window, it was my job to take care of it. I also took care of any woodworking to be done in the offices.

The Trip to Italy

We were preparing to build our new house on the Regattastrasse just a city block south from our Kiosk. The preliminary plans had been checked and approved by the building department, and we still needed to make some minor changes. They estimated another eight to ten months before all the plans and paperwork would be finalized, so I had a few months to enjoy my time at the Canoe Club. They had planned a trip to Italy that summer of 1958. We planned to camp for two weeks on a small uninhabited island on Italy's largest lake, Lago de Garda (Lake Garda). That meant I had to save my money for the upcoming trip, and try to earn extra money as well.

a stormy day at lake Garda from left to right Strich, Datsch and Ilse

The camping trip arrived quickly and before I knew it I was on the train to Italy. We left at night and boarded the local train from Wiesbaden to Frankfurt and from there the express train to Italy. The next stop was Munich, and I clearly remember that there was a Bratwurst stand on wheels at the platform. They also sold *Weisswurst*, a traditional Bavarian sausage that was cooked without grilling. It was new to me, so I bought one and enjoyed it very much. As I was standing there, my friends were yelling my name and saying that the train was leaving so I quickly got on. Well, we didn't depart very quickly, and the trip lasted through the night over the mountains in the Austrian and Italian Alps. The next morning, we arrived in northern Italy—Merano—and after a short stop we continued to Bolzano, another historic town. The final stop was Rovereto.

After our luggage was unloaded on the railway platform at the station, the stationmaster called a local farmer. He arrived with a wagon pulled by a single donkey to transport us to the nearby camping ground. It was slow-moving transportation, so all of us walked alongside since there was no space in the wagon. And after the long train ride, it was good to stretch your legs and get the blood circulating. After registering at the campground office, we set about pitching the tents so we could get organized with the rest of our luggage and settle down for the day. Since the campground was located on Garda Lake, there was a sandy beach where you could cool off in the clear water of the lake.

In the late afternoon, we finished putting our boats together. Since they were foldboats, it didn't take long to assemble them. After that, we were hungry and went to the campground's restaurant. I ordered spaghetti and meatballs.

At the time, meat was scarce so our dinner table had a large basket of fresh rolls—the same bread that was in the meatballs. The dinner was very good and it came with a large bottle of red wine. We got a little tipsy at that dinner, and we felt free to drink because the wine came with the meal.

The owner's daughter was about my age and, in my eyes, she was very pretty. After dinner, I was sitting with her and talking. She spoke German so there was no communication problem. As so it goes with young people, I was once again in love. After the last guest left and the place closed, I had to go to my tent and get a good night's sleep. In the morning, some of us went to the store to get bread and eggs for breakfast. I realized my money bag with all my money was gone. At the time, the currency I had was the Lira, and inflation was high so we all carried millions of Lira in our photo bags for safekeeping. We had so many bills that they wouldn't fit into our regular wallets. After a short time, I retraced my steps and realized I had been in the restaurant last, so I went back. Luckily, the young lady from the night before had seen the money bag and kept it safe for me.

Ilse, Sam and Datsch on the way to the camping place

After breakfast, we took down the tents and folded them in small packages so they would fit into our boats. After all the gear was stored away and the place was cleaned up, I had to say goodbye to my newfound friend as we would be gone for the next two weeks. I remember the young girl waving to us as we paddled away to the big Garda Lake. After lunch, we arrived at our destination. It was one of the two islands on the lake, and the only island you were allowed to camp on. It was a hilly and rocky place and just big enough for us to set up our five tents. After we settled in, there was nothing to hold us back from enjoying the wonderful blue waters of the Garda Lake.

Datsch at Lago di Garda

Since there were nine of us in the party, we had six boats—three two-seaters and three single ones. There were three couples—Emma and Inge, Heine and Ilse, Strich and Biene—and three single guys, Sam, Marshal, and myself (Datsch). I believe Sam had a tent for one person and I shared a tent with Marshal. The rest of the afternoon, me and some of the guys went cliff diving, jumping from about eight to ten feet above the water. But the real thrill was below where you could see different-colored fish between the coral and reef. What a sight. I had never gone swimming in such clear water or seen such beautiful life below the surface. It was a wonderful experience and you didn't realize how tiring it was since you were enchanted by your surroundings. It was the experience of a lifetime and I remembered it always. The first night on the island, I got a good night's sleep, and in the morning one or two of the guys crossed the lake and walked to the nearby town to buy some food for breakfast. I remember that none of us spoke Italian, so we had to gesture and point to the items we wanted. For instance, when I wanted to buy eggs, I did a sort of chicken dance and added some clucking. That way we got our food and had some fun at the same time. The following day, we went by bus to Verona, the place where the story of Romeo and Juliet had originated. After visiting the sights with all the statues and gardens, we went to the center of town. There was an open market with all kinds of goods. I started to buy some leather sandals and found out quickly that you expected to haggle. You don't pay the asking price; instead, you had to go lower and keep bargaining. This activity is expected until both parties come to agree on a final price. After I successfully made my purchase, I was the one who bargained for most of the rest of us. When we got back to our small island, it was late in the evening and we decided not to cook; instead, we crossed the lake to a nearby restaurant.

After we enjoyed our meal, we had some wine and made plans for the following days. I watched as three different Italian guys took turns dancing with one girl. As soon as one was finished, the next one started. I took this as a challenge. I waited until I could get the girl's attention and gestured to her that I wanted to dance, so after the next dance, she came halfway towards me and I got up and danced with her the rest of the evening. The local boys left after a while. My friends were concerned that the local boys might take a knife to our boats since they were lying there on the beach, but when we came out our boats were right where we left them. One interesting outcome of the night: the girl's father said, "Call me papa," and invited us for the next day to a tennis match at the hotel where they were staying.

But I was not too keen about that and was a no show. I was enjoying my stay at the island, including diving in the blue waters of Lake Garda. After about six days on the island, we packed up our tents and moved on with our boats to a regular camping ground. It was more civilized: they had running water and regular toilets, which the women on our team truly appreciated. The island didn't have facilities, and we had all tired of having to make a pit stop at a nearby restaurant.

After we arrived, we pitched our tents and got situated, but then we were to go food shopping. It looked like everybody wanted to go except Heine; he volunteered to stay behind and watch the tents and other belongings. In the past, we had two people stay behind at an open camping facility since there were five tents to be watched. But Heine said, "Just go, I'll be all right." It was a long walk to the next town so we were gone for quite some time. As we were coming back, we could see Heine standing at the edge of the road waiting for our arrival.

As we got settled in, Heine told us the story. He had had a visitor, a young soldier from the nearby military barracks. The soldier came by bicycle and was very friendly and he spoke a little German, so after a while they got more acquainted with each other. Heine showed him his expensive camera and other things he had. As the story goes, the soldier encouraged Heine to take his bicycle and go off to see if we were on our way back. So Heine took the bike and was looking for us but he returned without finding us. As soon as Heine returned, the soldier said he had to go, but that he would be back. But he never returned: he was gone, and so was all our stuff—gone forever (including, by the way, my pistol—it was a gas pistol that my mother had bought for self-protection during late nights at the kiosk.)

These things can happen at any place and any time, but all in all, we had a safe and enjoyable trip and returned home without any major incidents. The trip home was just about the same as the journey coming out: most of the gang just slept, since it was a night journey. And now we had our stories and adventures to tell in the clubhouse about our trip to Italy, as we sat at our reserved round table and enjoyed our local beer. About a month or so after our return from Italy, we got some good news—our construction permit had come through.

On the movie set "Das Brennende Gericht" (in English
"The Burning Court"), from left to right: Walter Giller,
Fritz Lang, Nadja Tiller, and Perette Pardier

When it was processed before the expected time, we
had a sudden change in plans. It was late in the year and we
hadn't started construction on the house until the spring
of 1959 since the danger of frost was always there. And it
was a long cold winter—we had the basement all dug out
before the cold started. Mother had the kiosk open only
during the week from 10:00 a.m. to 5:00 p.m. in the winter
since there was no weekend traffic on the promenade. And
most business came from the nearby factories for breakfast
and lunch in those winter months. I was still working on
weekends at the theater. One day as I got ready for a performance, I walked on stage and to my amazement I saw Mr.
Kling, my former boss and mentor from the apprentice-

ship years. We both looked at each other and asked, "What are you doing here?" I was surprised to learn that after he retired, he had to get a part-time job to make ends meet. He was in charge of opening and closing the curtains and other handyman work.

After working at the state theater for about two years, I decided to see if I could get into the movies, so I asked the stage manager what I had to do to work in a movie studio. He made some calls and got me an appointment at the studio called Under den Eichen. When I got there, the supervisor sent me to the woodshop. I made it clear that there had been a mistake in the communication. I was still working in the Rheinhuette and wasn't looking for a woodworking job. After this was cleared up, I went to the city of Wiesbaden and registered as a model and an extra in the movies. They took my profile pictures and they were added to my resume.

A man who worked in the office said that if I would build some shelves for his wife, he would get me work at the movies. I did all the shelving and got the work: we made advertising for Blaupunkt TV and for short and full-length films. One morning, we worked at the Frankfurter Airport to shoot a commercial for a German cigarette company. We started at 3:00 a.m. and had to be finished by 6:00, since the first plane arrived shortly after. These were enjoyable moments in my life since I got to play the leading man most of the time.

It wasn't easy to go back to the woodshop after all the movie work and all the attention I got. But as always, life goes on and we do our work to make money to pay our bills, and we cannot be too choosy about it. In the winter of 1958 to 1959, we had to get all our finances ready for the start of our new home. Mother spoke to the cement company to get the cement at a reasonable price, since my grandfather had worked for them for many years and my grandmother lived in a flat that belonged to the company. Mother promised to let grandmother live with us in to the new home so the flat could be returned to the company. We had to save in every way we could. The beer company gave us a loan and we paid it back—with each case of beer we sold, we paid an additional one Deutsche Mark until the loan was paid off.

My brother Joseph and I had to do all the work ourselves. My father was to do the masonry work since he never paid child support all those years. Otherwise, we never would have started this project, since building a house in Europe is pretty much all masonry work. The basement was below the frost line so we leveled the dirt floor and put the footing forms with reinforced steel rods in place. After all the footing was poured, we removed all the forms and started the basement walls forms with all the wood we had and the steel rods had to be put in place. As I said, my brother and I did most of this work. My father stopped by after work to check up on our work and gave his input, which was very important to our project. All work was done after work and on weekends. After the basement walls where poured in place, we did the ceiling next. It was concrete also. We placed railroad steel tracks about two feet apart on top of our basement walls and fastened our wooden forms with special hooks below the tracks.

The railroad tracks were part of the support for the concrete floor and stayed in place after we removed the forms.

We mixed the concrete by hand since we had no machine to do the job. At last, you could see a building starting to take shape. We started the concrete block walls. My father, my brother, and I did the first floor. My brother and I were the laborers. We mixed the cement and carried the cement blocks. By late summer, we prepared the first floor ceiling joist with heavy wood beams. The plan showed about two feet of concrete blocks above the floor for the second floor walls, but after Mother saw the low walls, she asked if we could add a few more blocks. So I started to put sixteen inches on top of the walls—two more blocks. Since the plan showed different, my father refused to do the job. And we didn't proceed without incident. One time I took my brother's moped scooter without asking and when he saw me driving away, he took a steel hammer and threw it at me, missing my head by just half an inch. Yes, my brother acted first and thought later in many situations. When we played cards as kids, if he lost, he flew into a rage and tore the cards to pieces.

The framer came and checked all the walls and started the roof rafters. There was a large dormer in the front facing the Rhine River and a smaller one in back of the house for the full bathroom. Each side had a one window dormer. It is tradition to put a pine tree on the framing of the roof before the tile roofing gets installed. Since it was just before Christmas, I got a pine tree and fastened it on top for good luck. It was about two weeks before Christmas Eve, and on Christmas Eve, Mother said that we needed a tree. So I went to our house under construction and I removed the pine tree. Some people saw me taking the tree from the rafters and thought I was stealing it.

During the winter months, we mainly cleaned the place on weekends since we had no time to clean during the week, as work came first. It gave us some free time. In my case, I worked at the movies as much as I could. In the spring of 1960, the roof tiles were delivered. Now this was a job by itself since it was a Hip Roof, a four-sided sloped roof, so all tiles on the four corners had to be cut. We had no saw for cutting glazed roof tiles so Father showed me how to cut the tile with a hammer. First you score the tile with a glass cutter break the glaze of the surface, and then you put it in the sand. You hammer the edges with a mason hammer and then tap lightly in the middle, trying not to break it in the wrong place—and of course that happened more than once.

Before we could install the roofing tiles, we had to mason the chimney through the roof rafters, and I hoped my father would do this since he had done the next door neighbor's chimney. My father made special chimneys in his days. He showed me the ones he did as a young man at the villa from Dykerhoff, the cement factory owner. As it happened, my father was too old and tired by then, so we got our chimney built just straight without any special work by a regular mason. On top of it all, we had to pay for all the extra mason work and buy him lunch and beer, since he worked on weekends. By spring 1960, all the windows were installed. I got the glass for a special price from the place where I worked, and then I had to install it. After the building was secured and the floor tiles were installed, I started on the interior doors and on building furniture for the store. Since we had a delicatessen, the street side had two big showcase windows with heavy wooden blinds that were pulled up in the morning and closed at night.

The interior furniture was a big job, so I had a friend help me. We made the showcase boxes, the main counter, the side cabinets to store liquor and other items, and a special shelf for the fresh rolls and bread we got delivered each morning. The store was open for business before we moved in to the living quarters since the kiosk had to be removed by a certain time—the city lease was up and would not be extended. One day, my sister Lilo was working in the store by herself until very late in the evening. Mother was worried and sent me to make sure she got home safely. On top of everything else, Lilo had to carry the day's earnings home with her.

Around this time, my older sister Erika and her husband came strolling by our new house and were suddenly taken with the idea of moving into the apartment upstairs. Even before we had started building the house, Mother had asked Erika and her husband Franz to get a bank loan to help out financially with the construction. So they were to have an apartment in the new home, but both of them laughed it off saying, "We already have a place to live." But after all the struggle to get the house built, they decided to move in upstairs. Since Franz came from the eastern part of Germany, he would have gotten a low interest rate loan and it would have taken a lot of pressure off Mother and the rest of us. Being a mother, she agreed to let them move in, and the only thing she requested was that they provide tile flooring and wallpaper. We finally moved into the new place in the spring of 1960. It was a busy year all around since my sister Lilo moved to America and Mother could no longer count on her help in the store.

My older sister Inge and her husband, Brenton F. Smith, were stationed in Texas, as he was in the air force at the time. Lilo visited them after staying in New York for a short time, where she met her future husband. After the Texas visit, Lilo returned to NY and got engaged to Fred Engelke. He was from the eastern part of Germany, which had been occupied by the Russian military, and he immigrated to America in 1955. Fred had an uncle in New York where he was staying before he entered the military. Fred served in the U.S. military for two years before he met my sister Lilo. After that, he worked as a house painter for a local contractor. Lilo and Fred got married at the German singing clubhouse in New Rochelle, New York in December 1961.

Yes, 1960 was still a busy year all around and there were still many unfinished items to be completed, like the stone wall around our property. I had to go to the quarry with the factory dump truck driver. We got rough stones and I had to cut them piece by piece to make them fit. After all the stones were in place, I put wooden forms in back and poured concrete between the forms and the stone. With reinforced steel rods, the final wall was two feet thick. (I am very proud of this masterpiece and have included a photo in this book.) At the beginning, my father did the layout for the wall structure, since it had a curve in it. We did not have too many weekends for ourselves anymore, but I remember one Saturday when my friends from the WKV came by as I was painting the hall in the new home and reminded me of a big event that night. It was a Eurovision

Television event in the Rhine Main hall center in the City of Wiesbaden.

My friends were free and had not committed themselves to a big job the way I had. After I completed my painting of the hallway, I got ready for the big event. In those days, you showered and put on a suit, especially on a Saturday night. I arrived late at the hall. So I told my friends I would meet them after the show. It was a concert with singers from all over Europe. I remember one of the German singers was Heidi Bruehl. She finished second in the contest behind a newcomer, Wyn Hoop. As I got to the box office, it was so late the ticket lady told me that it was sold out. So I started down the long hallway back to the exit and as I came to the swinging glass doors, I saw in the reflection a person waving behind me.

I turned around and saw the ticket lady waving something at me. I went back to the ticket counter and the lady told me there was one ticket left and sold it to me for two marks. As the usher escorted me with his flashlight, I couldn't believe how close we got to the front. The place was dark and I was in the front next to the stage, which was all lit up. He pointed to a seat—there was just one person in front and I was sitting next to him, all the seats in the front row were empty. I was sitting next to the mayor of the city of Wiesbaden and did not know it until the next day on Sunday. When I came into the clubhouse, the replay was on TV and I saw myself sitting next to the Mayor. I enjoyed the show, but everyone wanted to know how I had gotten a VIP ticket and how much it had cost. Some people said I had gotten the seat because I worked in the movies, but now I can finally reveal the truth in this book. I personally think it was just pure luck—the sun was shining on me, as the say.

After all the work on the house, I still had time to go and play in the movies. I worked for two weeks on a movie called *Das Brennende Gericht* (The Burning Courthouse). It was a French-German production and the main actors were Nadja Tiller, Jean-Claude Brialy, Walter Giller, Perette Pradier, Claude Rich, Edith Scob, and Duvalles.

The True Stories

The winter of 1959 to 1960 was unusually cold and there were ice patches floating in the Rhine River. This was during the Cold War between Russia and Western Europe. Since it got dark so early in the winter months, we didn't have much to do, given that there was no TV at the time. We listened to the radio and played board games. One I recall especially was called Mill. This game was mother's favorite since she was often the winner. She knew just how to set those chips and made the right moves every time. This leisure time is an important part of my story, since Mother and I spoke about the past and the present of our family.

One story I remember Mother telling was about a time when she was eighteen, in 1925, and was working for a British officer's family. This was in Wiesbaden in an apartment building with a variety of tenants. One day, Mother went for the mail in the foyer of the building and encountered a boy who was about twelve. She asked him who he was. The boy replied, "I am the grandson of Kaiser Wilhelm—yes, Kaiser Wilhelm is my grandfather." At the time, after the First World War, Kaiser Wilhelm was in living in exile in Holland. The Kaiser had six sons and one daughter and this boy was the daughter's son. The boy said that he and his mother were going to visit his grandfather in Holland on his school break.

I remember Mother telling me about my half-sisters, Inge and Erika. When she was twenty-three, Mother had been engaged to a young man. She ended up getting pregnant, but the young man had also impregnated another girl at the same time, and since he could only marry one, he chose, and it was the other girl. So by 1930, Mother was the unmarried mother of twin girls, and she went to live with our grandmother. Since the grandfather of the twins was an attorney, he made sure Mother was paid alimony. After a short time, Mother went back to work, and since these jobs were mostly live-in, grandmother was left to care for the two girls.

There was a time during the war when Mother, my sister Inge, and myself went to Karlsruhe to visit Father at the compound. (I told about this trip earlier in the book.) When we got there, a lady at the place where we were staying told Mother, "Your husband's cousin was here last week." At first, Mother was confused. Father didn't have any cousins living nearby. But the lady continued to explain: "The one with the red hair." Mother said, "Oh yes, now I know who you mean," but she was covering up the truth. The red-haired woman was Father's girlfriend. Now, many years later, she finally revealed the secret, (and I guess I am doing the same by writing about it here.)

My father had many affairs. The woman with red hair was his best friend's wife, and she had three children with him. She had four kids with her husband, so she had a total of seven kids to take care of. I remember going there as a child with my father, and the place was filthy—their mother didn't clean the way our mother did. So I had two half-sisters and a brother on Father's side. In later years, we saw them walking past us one day, but we ignored them. We had nothing in common with those kids and they had a different upbringing and lifestyle.

When I asked about Father and the final divorce, Mother told me that it was his lifestyle that broke the camel's back. There was no excuse for his behavior and the war was not a factor, since he had behaved in the same way before the war. I remember when he was telling his stories to his friends, and they were not very nice. One I recall was about a time when he visited a house of prostitution: he and his friend had their fun but afterwards they refused to pay. They tossed the furniture out the window and took off without paying. He liked to tell these stories in a bar that was his home away from home. At the time, we were living in the WKV and had the concessions for the bar and restaurant.

One night after the party was over, Mother was tallying up the receipts so we could pay for the deliveries that had been made the day before. The parties were held on Saturdays, so on Sunday the whole family pitched in to help clean up—except Father, who was sleeping it off, and who had taken most of the money out of the drawer when he left. After Mother confronted him, he just smiled and went on his way. That was just one of many things that led to the divorce.

In the spring of 1960, I got my driver's license, which was quite an expensive undertaking at the time. We had to save on all fronts to pay for it. One thing that made it just barely affordable was that I completed the minimum number of required hours and no more. At that time in Germany, you had to have a certain number of driving hours to get your license.

The year 1961 was full of surprises. We received a letter from my sister Lilo in America telling us about their plans. Mother was crying with happiness when she read the news, and all of us were extremely happy. Yes, my sister Lilo and her husband Fred planned to stay in Germany for three months. For one of those months, they planned to visit Fred's family in the eastern part of Germany.

One day in the spring of 1961, my friends Hans Deucker and his girlfriend Ilse Klee from the WKV came to our home. At the time, I asked how they met, and Ilse explained that after she turned eighteen, her brother, a dentist who was a member of the WKV at the time, let her use his paddleboat. After Ilse came back from her paddle tour, she had to clean the boat. She found a bucket and filled it with water, and at that moment Hans came and offered to carry the bucket.

Ilse told him, "I can carry the bucket myself."

This was their first encounter, and the rest is history. They got married a few years later. It was a good catch for both. Ilse is a very pretty tall young lady, and when she smiles, she has a sparkling gleam in her eye. And Hans is a dark-haired, tall, athletic, good-looking man. They were made for each other.

When they arrived, they had some news for me. Ilse had a girl friend from school who had a car and was unattached at the time. Her name was Lore and she was very nice. Since none of us had a car to get around, the deal was that if I liked the girl and she liked me, we would take weekend drives into the country. After our session, I agreed to go along, since Ilse was a good persuasive talker and was also very pretty. It was always a nice time to get away from everyday work. And at the time, I looked forward to a change of scenery on the weekends. In a few hours, we drove to towns that, when we were kids, had taken us days to reach by bicycle, and the memory stayed with you. But in the long run there was no spark between myself and Lore, and the car rides came to an end.

Franz Dinewitzer's son Edwin had a Vespa scooter, and sometimes on Saturday nights, I would ride on the back of it with him to Wiesbaden for the night. That was okay in good weather, but I had better times on weekends in the country with my sister Marianne. Out in the country, people knew each other and came together in the town sports center. There was music and dancing once a month or more, depending on the season. Most of the people were farmers who had to work the fields, but after the last harvest was done, the farmers had more leisure time, and they would tinker with machinery or repair old barns. Since I came from "the big city," as they called it, the girls liked that and were more cheerful towards me. So many weekends, I danced the whole night through and I came home with good memories. The one hitch was that you had to take few different bus lines to get to the town of Holzhausen a.d. Haide, where my sister lived. But I was young then, so I didn't mind at all. This was in late 1961 and early 1962, and my sister Liselotte and her husband Fred would be arriving that summer.

The Home coming Lilo and Fred

A s their arrival neared, Mother was more excited than anyone, or maybe it was just that she was the most demonstrative. Two of my sisters were in the U.S. at that time. One in Georgia and one in New York. In 1952, Ingeborg left Germany to come to Georgia as a nineteen-year-old bride with her husband, Fred Smith. I remember one story Ingeborg told us years later about when she had first come to the States. She didn't have a driver's license and had to take a bus to get around. In those days, they had the front seats for white people and the back was for black people. But Ingeborg didn't know the rules and went straight to the back of the bus to find a seat. Before long, a white person yelled "nigger lover" at my sister, who was placidly sitting in the back with no clue about what was going on. This is the kind of thing that can happen when you're a newcomer and don't know the rules and regulations. As the years went on, both of my sisters gained a lot more knowledge and experience about how the American people lived.

In the meantime, we got an update from Liselotte about when she would be arriving. She was coming on July 6, 1962 on Pan American. We still had a month before they arrived, and there was a lot to get ready before then. Some of the exterior woodwork had to be painted, like the windows, the soffits, and fascia boards before the gutters and leaders could to be installed. The house was ready for us to stucco the exterior, but we didn't have the money to do it. I was still working at the factory and we got news that the management was looking to house immigrants from Spain, many of whom were working temporarily in Germany. But our first priority was to get the room ready for my sister and her husband, so I made a door for one of the basement rooms that faced the lawn and the Rhine. We painted the walls and ceiling and put in a plywood floor for a bedroom where I and my brother Josef would sleep. We finished the work on my upstairs bedroom so it would be ready for Liselotte and Fred. It was a great time to have an older brother around. Technically, he was my brother-in-law but I looked up to him like a brother. Plus, I was thrilled to have my darling sister around, as I had missed her very much.

They had planned to rent a car for their stay in Germany, since Fred came from the Eastern bloc of Germany, and it was better if they had a car. But after a few days in Germany, he decided against the car rental. He told us that he would pay for the paint for the house after we had completed the stucco (rough cast) work. So we set about getting a quote for the stucco. After an extended search, we found a young journeyman who would do the work, and Fred negotiated it. He insisted on a fixed price for the labor and materials, and after it was completed satisfactorily, Fred got the great idea to buy the paint and add it to the cement mix. After the house was stuccoed, we no longer needed to paint. This job still looks great more than fifty years later.

House under construction

House complete

This adventure of the house was making a big dent in Fred's wallet, but he and my sister were good-natured about it, and instead of renting a car, they explored by bicycle. If I remember correctly, the bicycle tour was not much fun. One day my sister's sandal came apart, and since they had only taken a bit of money for the ride, they ended up buying a pair of wooden sandals, which gave my sister blisters. To make matters worse, they were about twenty-four kilometers from home on a hot summer day, their water supply ran low, and they didn't have any money left to buy something to drink. Needless to say, Fred and Liselotte came home exhausted. In the next few days, they did a better job of securing appropriate gear, and they enjoyed the local day tours much more. Fred had brought an 8 mm movie camera and a projector with him. As I was still working at the movie studios then, he let me take the camera and I made a short movie on the set from the commercial we made. Since the electric is a different current in Europe, we got a convertor to run the projector and charge the battery for the movie camera.

After he showed movies from his hometown in New York, he told me, "If you want to pay off the mortgage on the house faster, you can come to the U.S. for a year and raise enough money to pay all your bills." This was the start of all that followed. It was a big decision at the time. We talked about the time Fred left Germany and came to America. His Uncle Gustaf sponsored Fred to come over in 1955. You had to be a citizen in good standing for seven years and have security in order to vouch for someone else. In my case, Fred would give the security statement to the

American Consulate, which was located in Frankfurt am Main, about thirty miles from my home.

After a long talk with my mother and Fred, I decided to try it for a year. Fred kept saying, "Just go for a year and if you don't like it, you can always go home." So I started to get my paperwork together, which meant many trips to Frankfurt and to the American Consulate.

After a while, Fred and Liselotte went to East Germany to visit Fred's father, stepmother, and brother, plus his older brother, wife, and kids. All of them lived in Leipzig, in East Germany, under Russian communist rule. It was quite difficult to enter the eastern sector because you had to pass through Checkpoint Charlie by foot or car. And if you travelled by train, after you entered the eastern sector, the train came to a full stop. Soldiers with guns would board and search the train. Fred had to leave their compartment and go to the luggage compartment, where they searched his suitcases. If Fred and Liselotte were invited by a cousin or aunt to visit, they had to log the address in a daybook before they left the house. Since they were registered via the father's address, they had to sign out and log in the address where they were visiting, in case the local police needed to implement any controls. In those days it was not easy to live in East Germany.

Months started to fly by, and I had a lot to do before I could depart on December 5, 1962, the day my ship would sail. I sold my paddleboat, my pride and joy, and gave notice at the factory. It was still summer and Fred and Liselotte came back from East Germany with lots of stories and new experiences. Fred sponsored quite a few people, one of whom, Wolfgang Kuhn, I met in Germany.

He had enlisted in the military before immigrating to the U.S. and was living in Berlin. As it happened, one weekend, Wolfgang was on military leave and came to our place for a visit. It was the weekend we had planned to stay with my sister Marianne, and as I recall, we rented a car and drove out to the country to the town of Holzhausen, where there were some nice old-fashioned restaurants and bars. We met Wolfgang at an old train station, which had been converted into a restaurant and bar. It was a cozy place for guys to get together for a drink. Wolfgang talked about the military and his life in the States. I don't remember any of our conversation but I do remember drinking beer with a Jägermeister chaser, a combination that will knock you out. I slept over that night at my sister Marianne's place, and she said I talked in my sleep, saying, "America, America," over and over. I guess all the talk of the States combined with the alcohol made a perfect mix for a dream.

The next day was Monday, and Wolfgang had to go back to the military. We went home to tend to business. I wasn't employed at the time, and was looking for a temporary job for the next four months. After a search, I found what I was looking for at a brick manufacturing company. My job was to sort the good bricks from the bad. The "bad" ones had gotten too hot and were bent out of shape. I made as much there, or more, than I had at the factory, depending on how many hours I put in. For this kind of work, you needed special gloves, which were provided by the factory; without those gloves you'd have no fingerprints left by the end of the day. The good thing about this job was that you could come and go as you pleased, and it was piecework, so you got paid by the amount of bricks you separated out. I sold my paddleboat to a friend in the neighbor-hood, and built an overseas trunk for my clothing and my other belongings. I had some German books and some of my veneer pictures. When you have limited space in your trunk, it's a sure way to figure out what you have of value.

The Journey Across the Pond

As the days flowed by and we quietly went about our daily routine, I began to realize how precious life actually is. Usually, we notice this sort of thing more as we get older. The day approached when my sister and brother-in-law were planning their trip home. We had had some good times and shared a lot of memories. I recall one of Fred's stories. He was about twelve and living in East Germany in the Russian sector. His job was to drive the Russian children to school in a horse-drawn buggy, which was a farmer's old wooden ladder wagon. Fred had to get up very early in the morning to get the horse and wagon ready to drive the children to school, and he did. This lasted for about three years. Then when he turned fourteen, he began an apprenticeship as a painter. After three years, he became a journeyman and he worked for another year for his boss. When he applied for a visa to visit his sister in the western part of Germany, he easily got it since he had a clean past. Once Fred arrived in the western part of Germany, he knew there was no going back to the eastern bloc. He contacted his Uncle Gustav in New York and applied for a visa and his uncle sponsored him. He sailed for New York in 1955 on a German ship called *Berlin*. Before his journey overseas, he contacted his father once more for a last visit, and gave him most of the money he had saved, since they didn't have much at that time.

When Fred and Lilo left to return to the States, it was a wet goodbye—and I don't mean that it was rainy. No, it was simply that a lot of teardrops fell—both mother and daughter were crying. Eventually, time healed both of them the way time heals most everything. We made a lot of phone calls to the States and the exchanges were more direct, not the way they used to be years ago when Mother would call my sister Ingeborg and they'd spend most of the time crying. Since it was quite expensive to place a transatlantic call in those days, you had to have your act together and know what to say.

I now had to present papers to the U.S. Consulate, so I had to wait for a bank statement from Fred to arrive for the final paperwork to be completed. In September 1962, the letter arrived from the First Westchester National Bank of New Rochelle, New York. It stated that Fred Engelke had had an interest-bearing account with the bank since November 1960. This sworn statement was all we needed to present to the Consulate. On October 13, I made my final trip to the U.S. Consulate and got the visa I needed to enter the U.S. Along with my visa, I got a booklet: The Constitution of the United States of America, dated October 13, 1962.

In the meantime, a new tenant moved in to our home. We needed the extra money to pay the bank loan, since I would be gone soon. Mother had to make ends meet, so we took in six people from Spain as temporary tenants. It was not easy to communicate in the beginning since none of us spoke Spanish, and the Spaniards did not speak German.

They worked at the factory and made themselves understood mostly via hand gestures. After a few weeks, I went out with the younger Spanish men on weekends to local restaurants and bars, so I learned the language quickly and was able to communicate with the tenants. In a short time, I spoke Spanish very well and they spoke pretty good German.

If only my English could have been as good, but I had no one to speak the language to. In just two months, I would be in another country across the pond. On December 12th, I would arrive in New York harbor. Mother purchased items for my overseas trunk and I bought two new suitcases, a new suit, and a hat. I had no idea that nobody really wore suits and hats even in those days, except if you worked in an office where you had a dress code. As my departure neared, I arranged to put everything I wasn't taking into storage in the basement and the attic. It was no big deal, since I was going only for a year or so. Yes, this was our deal. I was a loyal German citizen and proud of it, even though in the back of my mind I knew it would take longer, since Fred mentioned that most people stayed for two years. I did one more advertisement in the movie studio in November and told them I would be gone for about a year.

Then on December 4th I left my house to go to the train in Wiesbaden. My mother had a head cold, so I said goodbye and left, and my brother Josef came along since I had two suitcases and an attaché case. We took the local bus to the train station in Wiesbaden and said goodbye there. I took the train to Frankfurt am Main, and there took a special train to Bremen, and from there took a bus to get to the harbor. Before the final bus, we had breakfast in a local restaurant. I don't remember for sure what was on the menu, but the usual breakfast was a soft boiled egg, buttered roll, milk, hot chocolate, coffee or tea. After breakfast, the bus took us to the harbor. There was the biggest ship I had ever seen right in front of me, and no mistaking that it was the right one, as it said, *S. S. Bremen*. People were lined up by the hundreds and it was slow going. At check-in, I remember a young woman with her five-year-old daughter and the grandmother. The older lady asked me if I was boarding the ship, and when I said yes, she asked me to watch out for her daughter and the child. I said I would. After boarding, you saw everybody and nobody. I was standing at the rail looking down as the big band played a German song about a young man leaving his town behind, and I could see that many people had tears in their eyes.

We boarded as scheduled between 8:00 and 11:00 a.m., and after three hours the ship was completely loaded and all the excitement had quieted down. I went to my cabin and found that I was sharing with two roommates, so there were three of us in my cabin. One was a young man about my age and the other was someone in his fifties. After I familiarized myself somewhat with the ship, an announcement came over the loudspeaker that our departure was delayed due to fog. The next stop was Southampton, in England, and there was heavy fog over the North Sea that connected with the English Channel. Later in the evening, we heard an announcement that the ship would arrive one day later than scheduled, and if anyone wanted to make a call, we could do so at the ship's phone service. I was one of the first in line to place a call to my mother to let her know about the delay. But I couldn't reach her. Only later did I learn that her cold had gotten worse, so she'd gone to bed early and wrapped heavy wool scarves around her head, and she couldn't hear the phone. When I was in the room making the call, I met a man in his sixties named Robert Janchens, a retired opera singer who had performed at the Metropolitan Opera in New York City. We had a conversation about the theater, studios, and movies I had been in.

In 1962, he had gone to Germany to get married. Forty years earlier, when he was a young man, his father was the captain of a German passenger ship traveling from Germany to New York on a regular schedule. One day, Robert, the then-young opera singer (who was called Bob), left the ship in New York and didn't return. He made his living singing in different places until he got the break he needed to sing at the Metropolitan Opera. When he was traveling with his father as a young man, he had met a young lady who was about fifteen years younger than he was. She was travelling with her father, who was a salesperson for a German company. Since Bob was the captain's son, the businessman and his daughter knew about him. And Bob stayed in contact with the young lady throughout the years.

The next day, I ended up meeting the young lady, who was Bob's new wife. She was about fifty now and had a son who was twelve. And all this in one day! It looked like the trip would be anything but boring. As soon I saw Bob, he called out to me, "It's Lang from Wiesbaden," and he and I had to have a beer and a Steinhäger, which is a schnapps from Germany.

Bob the Opera Singer

Dinner

Tomato Cocktail

Asparagus Cream Soup

Fried Sea-salmon Lyonnaise
Emma Salad

Braised Philadelphia Capon Marengo
Cauliflower Polonaise   Fondantes Potatoes
Lettuce Salad   Dill Dressing

Chocolate Ice Cream, Wafers

Fresh Fruit in Season

Coffee

For Children   Sago in Milk with Biscuit

To Order

Soups   Ham Purée Soup Dolgoruki
               Chicken Broth in Cup

Fish   Poached Halibut, Sauce Hollandaise

Entrées   Fried Calf's Liver with Bacon
                   Fresh Spinach in Cream   Roasted Potatoes
               Smoked Tenderloin of Pork, Burgundy Sauce

Salads   Chicory   Tomato   Cucumber   Pepper

Dressings   Lorenzo   Escoffier   Herb   Ketchup

Vegetables   Nantaise Carrots   Green Peas
                   Broccoli   Lima Beans

Potatoes   Boiled   Mashed   Vauban   Pommes frites

Dessert   Rice Condé   Coconut Meringue Pie

Cheese   Assorted Cheese - Crackers - Radishes

Beverages   Coffee - Tea - Kaffee Hag
               Peppermint - Camomile

10.00 p. m.   Sandwiches

S.S. »BREMEN«   Wednesday, December 5th, 1962

135

Lunch

Russian Salad - Spanish Fish Salad - Sea Salmon in Oil - Gabelbissen
Eggs with Anchovies - Fried Herring - Matie Fillet in Sour Cream
Ripe and Green Olives - Table Celery

Green Pea Soup Bourgeoise

Fried Plaice, Lime Butter
Mayonnaise Salad

Chopped Beefsteak with Onions
Braised Celery en Branches Bordelaise   Roasted Potatoes
Lettuce Salad, St.-Regis Dressing

Woodruff Crystal Jelly

Fresh Fruit in Season

Coffee

To Order

Soups	Danish Duckling Soup
	Consommé Double in Cup
Fish	Boiled Haddock, Dill Sauce
Entrées	Pork and Beans Boston Style
	Spaghetti Caruso, Parmesan
Cold Dishes	Home-made Liver Pâté, Sauce Oxford
	Assorted Cold Roast, Indian Relish
	Choice of Fresh and Smoked Sausage
Salads	Escarole Tomato Combination Red Beet
Dressings	Rudolph's Chiffonade Chervil Chili
Vegetables	Young Carrots Fried Egg-plant
	Cauliflower Courgettes Bretonne
Potatoes	Boiled Mashed Baked Idaho German Fried
Dessert	Chocolate Ice Cream, Wafers
	Stewed Apples
Cheese	Danoise Camembert Harzer Milkana
	Coffee - Tea - Cacao - Kaffee Hag
	Peppermint - Camomile
4.00 p. m.	Coffee - Tea - Cake

S. S. "BREMEN"   Wednesday, December 12th, 1962

Nightclub party on the Bremen Fritz is wearing the hat

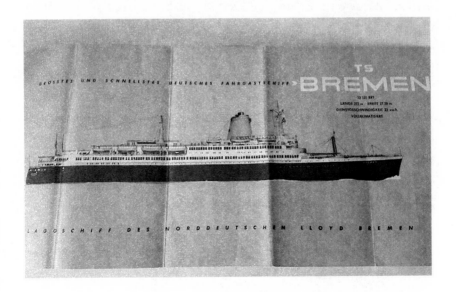

This and more happened on my journey across the pond. One day, Bob invited me for dinner with the captain. But there was one catch: I had no dark suit in my suitcase—it was in the trunk in the bottom of the ship's hull. I spoke to my steward and he said there was no problem. He forwarded the request to the deckhands, who asked me to come downstairs to the ship's storage area to point out the trunk. They quickly found the trunk and after I unlocked it and retrieved my dark suit, I had to show my appreciation. So I went to their cantina to buy them a few drinks. The sailors' bar was quite a ways below the main deck. A narrow winding staircase led to their quarters. The drinks were inexpensive and weren't the main thing, anyway. What the sailors really liked was to be able to talk to a passenger, since they worked many hours to make the ship run smoothly.

All these things you learn over the course of your life's journey if you're willing to accept and register it in your brain. Yes, people need people to talk, listen, and accept each other. This is the key to a smooth, good, clean, healthy life.

As for my roommates, the only time I saw them was very briefly at night when I went to bed, since they were both seasick most of the time. It never even occurred to me that I would be seasick and I had no time to think about it, since there was always something to do. It's true that the sea was quite rough and the glass doors by the railing were closed for the entire journey. At one time, I saw four young men running around the ship yelling, "Iceberg!" but everyone ignored them.

I have transcribed the daily activity program below:

Today's Program, Thursday, December 6th, 1962 Tourist Class—S. S. >> Bremen
7:00 a.m. Holy Mass   Theatre, P-Deck

Celebrated by Rev. Studienrat Paul Wermers
7:30 a.m. Breakfast (1st Seating)   8:30 a.m. Breakfast (2nd Seating)
8:15 a.m. Protestant Morning Service   Theatre, P-Deck

Conducted by Rev. Walter Lueck
9:30 a.m. Motion Picture: "Freddy und der Millionaire," starring Freddy Quinn and Heinz
Erhardt. Short Feature: "Ex Voto"   Theatre, P-Deck

10:00 a.m. Horse Races Veranda, P-Deck
10:30 a.m. Brass Music Promenade Deck

With the complete "Bremen" Orchestra
11:30 a.m. Lunch (1st Seating)   1:00 p.m. Lunch (2nd Seating)
3:00 p.m. Partners for Games   Passengers who want to meet partners for card games, deck games, conversation, etc. are kindly requested to call at the Card Room at 3:00 p.m.   Special Travel Service.

4:00 p.m. Coffee (1st Seating)   4:30 p.m. Coffee (2nd Seating)
4:00 to 6:00 p.m. and 7:30 to 10:00 p.m. Dancing to the tunes of the Jukebox on the Veranda

4:30 p.m. Concert   Main Lounge, P-Deck
4:30 p.m. Bingo   Smoking Room, P-Deck
5:00 p.m. Rosary   Tavern, E-Deck
6:00 p.m. Dinner (1st Seating)   7:30 p.m. Dinner (2nd Seating)
8:30 p.m. Musical Bouquet   Main Lounge, P-Deck
9:00 p.m. Motion Picture: "Who's Got the Action?" starring Dean Martin and Lana Turner; Short Feature: "Starting from Hatch"
Theatre, P-Deck

10:00 p.m. Sandwiches at the Lounge Smoking Room, Veranda, Tavern
10: 00 p.m. to 2:00 a.m. Gaiety goes on   Tavern, E Deck

This was the scope of daily activities and goings on. If the night life went late, I was lucky to get to the late sitting for breakfast. It wasn't quite as easy as it looked to be a young passenger on the ship full of fun. I wasn't used to this type of service every day and it took a while to get used to all that attention. In the daily program, it was printed that "The clock will be set back one hour every day." The swimming pool was open from 7:00 a.m. to 11:30 a.m. and again from 2:00 p.m. until 6:00 p.m. You could also go to the steam bath and if you had the money, you could make an appointment for a massage.

One evening, I was invited to eat with Bob and his new wife at the captain's table. It was a special treat to be sitting at the captain's table. I was introduced to the captain as "Lang from Wiesbaden," and Bob mentioned my movie experience. This was the start of a new conversation for the table. At the time, I didn't realize that new conversational topics were always in demand at the captain's table, and I was one of those who could make the evening more interesting and exciting. The captain, Guenther Roessing, was an all-around fun guy, and the evening ended with all of us in a very good humor. The next day, I got a note to come to the purser's office. I had no idea what the request was all about, but when I got there the purser had me sign some papers and handed me $40.00. I checked the document and saw my brother-in-law's name—Fred Engelke. He had sent me $40.00 as a backup, since he knew what it was like not to have any spending money. There was a note informing me of my new arrival date—the 13th of December, not the 12th, as had been planned earlier.

It was the fourth day on the Atlantic. My cabin was on A-Deck, Room # 221, an outside cabin, on the seventh deck up from the bottom and four below the top deck, which was the sports deck. My cabin was about forty feet, or twelve meters, above the waterline. The total distance from the sun deck to the waterline was seventy feet or twenty-one meters. In those days, the S.S. Bremen was considered a big ship—212 meters long and 27.50 meters wide, the biggest and fastest German passenger ship at the time, with a total of eleven decks, plus the storage rooms.

With each passing day I got to know more people and made more friends. I had a Zeiss Ikon camera, so I took a lot of pictures of Bob and his wife. I had received it as a going away present from my father, and it was quite old, so I had it checked before I left. I ended up spending a lot of money to have it repaired. Little did I know that they hadn't repaired it at all. It wasn't until I had the pictures developed that I realized there were no pictures. This was a great embarrassment for me, and Bob and his wife were quite disappointed, since we had spent a lot of time together taking all those pictures and poses. Oh well, like many things in life, it doesn't seem that important anymore.

The day of our parting was soon upon us. We had had such a great experience, one that happens only once in a lifetime. The night before our departure, the 12th of December, 1962, it was cloudy. As we approached the Port of New York City, you could see a light in the distance in the dark night. And as we came closer, we saw that the light was none other than the Statue of Liberty. It made a lasting impression on me and my fellow passengers.

The night before, December 11, there had been a full moon, and the activities were still going strong. The Tavern was open, as always, from 10:00 p.m. to 2:00 a.m., and the daily booklet claimed that your dance partner was waiting for you. And once again, we danced 'til the wee hours of the morning. After the second seating for breakfast, I took my daily walk around the ship and said goodbye to the people I might not see the next day. The fun was over and we would be disembarking after breakfast the next day, December 13, 1962.

The day before we departed was kind of a quiet laid-back day for most of us, since for many, including me, it was a step into the unknown. One good thing was that my sister and brother-in-law were waiting to welcome me. The Chief Steward, Fritz Raschke, gave us instructions for a smooth departure, including the time and place to be, since all paperwork had to be checked. After I had packed, I went to bed early, skipping the late night partying. In the morning, the line for the early breakfast was quite long, since everybody had the same idea. There was plenty of time, since nobody disembarked before 12:00 noon. I took my daily deck walk before breakfast and with each lap, the line for breakfast dwindled.

After breakfast, new lines formed, this time for visa and passport control. When it was my turn, I got my suitcase and overcoat and went to the designated destination and stood in line with the rest of the gang. It took about an hour and a half to get through the line. All my paperwork was in order and I was ready to see Liselotte and Fred. Yes, this was it. I was still on German soil, so to speak, but I was about to take the final step into the land of boundless opportunity. I wasn't afraid, but I was a bit skeptical about the "new world," as it was called.

As I disembarked, I looked over to my right to see someone waving in the distance from the upper deck of the ship. It was my new friend Bob hanging over the midship rail and waving a final goodbye. For Bob, it took longer to disembark since he had a car to be unloaded. So I gave him a quick wave and kept going to the exit for my final steps into the new world.

The End